Michael Doe

SEEKING THE TRUTH
IN LOVE

The Church and Homosexuality

DARTON·LONGMAN+TODD

First published in 2000 by
Darton, Longman and Todd Ltd
1 Spencer Court
140–142 Wandsworth High Street
London SW18 4JJ

ISBN 0–232–52399–1

A catalogue record for this book is available from the
British Library.

Phototypeset by Intype, London
Printed and bound in Great Britain by
Page Bros, Norwich, Norfolk

Contents

SEEKING THE TRUTH IN LOVE

Foreword

The Anglican Church's convictions about human sexuality continue to be an area of conflict and concern; for a significant number of Anglicans, this has come to be the acid test of whether you are inside or outside the pale of authentic orthodoxy. And for such people, even to allow that it is an area in which Christians might just possibly disagree without fracturing the reality of a common language is to betray the essential principle. We need reminding at times that there are other issues of sharp disagreement with which we have come to live. It may be that the prominence we currently give to questions of sexual ethics is itself a mark of how we are all affected by the obsessions of contemporary Western society; and if so, there are a few questions we ought all to be putting to ourselves before turning on each other, whether we think of ourselves as 'liberal' or 'traditionalist'.

This book is an attempt, as Bishop Michael puts it, to do something of what the 1998 Lambeth Conference in its plenary session on the subject didn't and perhaps couldn't do – to take some time in theological reflection on the background of the sexuality debate, and to ask some awkward questions about its historical and cultural setting. There is no suggestion here that all the weight falls on one side of the argument; but there is a strong plea for recognition that Christian ethics, while it is emphatically not the slave of its cultural context, needs some self-awareness in regard to that context. One of this book's virtues is that it does not pretend that there are simply two mutually exclusive perspectives on the question of same-sex relations in contemporary Anglicanism. I hope that it will provide some material and some stimulus for a more patient and (dare I say?) a more adult discussion than we have sometimes had of late. It digests a great deal of evidence and theory with enormous clarity, and deserves a wide welcome.

Rowan Williams
ARCHBISHOP OF WALES

Introduction

Bishops in Conference

'If we listen to these people,' shouted the bishop next to me, 'it'll be those who do it with animals next!' It was the opening session of one of the sections at the 1998 Lambeth Conference, the ten-yearly meeting of Anglican bishops from across the world. The motto of the Anglican Communion is 'The truth shall set you free'. The title of our section, one of four, was: 'Called to Full Humanity'.

The task of our sub-section was to consider the issue of Human Sexuality. What should the Church be doing? What should the Church be teaching – and especially where homosexuality was concerned? The outburst from the African bishop was his angry response to the suggestion that we should invite a group of gay and lesbian Christians to share their experience. The vote went against them being allowed in, and already it was clear how emotionally charged and potentially divisive this issue was going to be.

Over the next two weeks we worked together under the patient leadership of a South African bishop who knew all about seeking reconciliation in a divided community. Meeting in small groups, we shared our experience. I found myself with a Nigerian who believed gay people needed divine healing, a bishop who said they didn't have homosexuals in Papua New Guinea, an American who allowed clergy to live together in same-sex unions as long as they

were open with him about it and told him if their relationship broke up, and an Australian from Sydney who was
very clear that Scripture said 'No' and that was it.

Remarkably, a report emerged to which all the bishops
present finally agreed.[1] This was due in no small part to
the diplomatic skills of some Church of England bishops
whose own report, 'Issues in Human Sexuality',[2] had suc-
ceeded in holding different views together, or at least
holding the ground, in this country. Unfortunately, at
Lambeth matters did not end there. In addition to the
report, a resolution was needed for the Conference as a
whole to debate. Again, a process of working and praying
together enabled the sub-section to produce a draft to
which everyone could also agree. An American bishop not
normally known for his powers of conciliation led the group
in a hymn of praise!

Both the report and the draft resolution admitted that,
despite many things on which we could agree, Anglican
bishops held a variety of positions on the issue of homosexuality and we needed to accept that and continue to talk
and listen to each other. The Conference plenary was not
willing to be so tolerant, especially those bishops who had
met at Kuala Lumpur a few months earlier and come to
Lambeth with the express agenda of resisting what they saw
as the liberal tendency.

'This is not gay-bashing,' said the Bishop of Lahore,
addressing the plenary, 'but for us it's a matter of conscience, faith, doctrine and dogma.' From the other side,
David Crawley, Archbishop of Kootenay (Canada),
regretted that a resolution 'whose face, though conservative, was a face of love and compassion has been turned
into a face of judgement and condemnation'. By a large
majority the Conference declared that homosexual practice

was 'incompatible with Scripture' and could find no justification for the blessing of same-sex unions or the ordination of those involved in them. Scripture required either lifelong heterosexual marriage or singleness: a call to 'Chastity' was changed to 'Abstinence' lest there be any suggestion that permanent, faithful same-sex unions were exempt.[3]

The response was predictable. The media headlines read: 'Anti-gay bishops crush liberals' and 'Bishops defeat gay activists'; and their day was made when a press photographer happened to be on the spot when a Nigerian bishop attempted to 'exorcise' the General Secretary of the (British) Lesbian and Gay Christian Movement.[4]

On the other side, gay Christians spoke of their anger and rejection and their supporters disowned the resolution. 'In an effort to appease militant forms of Islam, particularly in Africa, the bishops abandoned gay and lesbian Christians . . . It was a modern form of human sacrifice.' Michael Ingham, Bishop of New Westminster (Canada).[5]

From the middle ground, there was some relief that the Conference had not completely endorsed the position wanted by the most conservative bishops in the so-called Kuala Lumpur Statement. The report of the sub-section was intact, and even the resolution called for more dialogue and debate throughout the Communion, and within this a call to 'listen to the experience of homosexual people'.

What was also significant in the final resolution was the assurance given to gay and lesbian people that 'they are loved by God and that all baptised, believing and faithful persons, regardless of sexual orientation, are full members of the Body of Christ'. Immediately after the final plenary some of the bishops prepared a Pastoral Letter to Lesbian and Gay Anglicans – since signed by nearly two hundred of us – regretting any sense of rejection caused by the Conference's inability to hear their voices.

Lambeth 98 was an insight into the richness and diversity of the worldwide Church, and how our differences can be both stimulating and disturbing. For me, that has been deepened by first-hand visits in the months that have followed, first to Uganda and then to North America. This book tries to share and reflect on that experience.

It also takes up some of the issues that Lambeth raised. Is it true to say that homosexual practice is incompatible with Scripture, and how does that fit with the way that the Church, and particularly Anglicans, come to conclusions about Christian truth? What does it mean to accept the homosexual orientation, to say that these people are full members of the Church, but to forbid them any expression of who they are? How does the experience of gay and lesbian people affect our understanding of sexuality in general? How should we understand 'same-sex unions' in relation to both Christian marriage and the sexual free-for-all which Western society has seemingly embraced?

The limitations of the book will soon become clear. It is written 'about' people, not by the people themselves. It is written by a man, and although, as the later chapters show, I am aware of the critical significance of feminist theology in the current debate, I don't pretend to do it justice. I also acknowledge that it's weaker on lesbianism than on male homosexuality, and hardly touches on the issues of bisexual or transgendered people.

It does not pretend to be a scholarly work, and the footnotes will direct readers to the sources from which I have myself drawn. I am grateful for the sabbatical leave which enabled me to read more widely in and around the subject, and especially for the hospitality of the Church Divinity

School of the Pacific (Berkeley, California) where I spent the first month. But the origins and aims of this work lie primarily in the pastoral field, in trying to help the Church to be more aware, more honest and more inclusive, as it grapples with these difficult questions.

This book is offered as a small contribution to the ongoing discussion of these difficult and, sadly, divisive issues within our Church. I hope I have listened fairly to the very different voices of those engaged in the intellectual and the pastoral pursuit of what God is trying to tell his Church at this time. What I have also tried to do is to listen to gay and lesbian people themselves. They are part of the Church, but the fear and hostility which surrounds them means that their voice is still rarely heard. Yet it is their lives and their faith that are at stake. I also believe that in the exploration and struggle to come to terms with these issues, the Church as a whole may learn more about what it is to be faithful to where God is today, about what it means to be the Body of Christ in our kind of world.

1

Around the Anglican Communion

The Lambeth resolution condemning homosexuality was seen as a victory for those who call themselves the 'traditionalists' in the Anglican Communion. Their greatest strength lies in those countries, particularly in Africa and Asia, once dominated by the churches who first sent them missionaries, but now finding their own voice. Their present support, including considerable financial aid, comes from the more conservative parts of the Episcopal Church in the USA and in Australia, and from certain parts of Latin America.

Africa

Within Africa, South Africa is the exception. The debate in the Province of South Africa has taken place against a background of political change resulting in a Bill of Rights which – for the first time in any nation's constitution – has included 'sexual orientation' amongst the protected categories.[1] The 'liberation theology' which has played such a central part in creating the new South Africa has for many

linked the oppression of black people with that of gays and
lesbians. 'I do not expect mainstream Christians to make a
public confession of sin and guilt, such as they had to make
for apartheid, yet nevertheless I believe that they will feel
the need to do so.'[2]

The Province's 1995 statement on 'The Church and
Human Sexuality' seeks to draw from the twin biblical
foundations of God's loving-kindness and God's righteous-
ness a 'Christian sexual ethic of love [which] arises from
faith's perception of God's ways with humankind'. It sees
this in his creativity, reconciliation and the way he liberates
human beings so that we may live with justice and integrity.
The aim of human relationships is therefore seen as mutual
commitment between partners which is faithful and life-
giving, rejecting domination and submission, but rather
seeking the enrichment of the other.[3]

> The Church's position is that sex is for life-long marriage
> with a person of the opposite sex, for the purposes of
> companionship, sexual fulfilment and procreation. The
> reality is that divorce and remarriage, polygamy, same
> sex unions, single parent families, and persons living
> together outside marriage do exist. As a church we have
> to find loving, pastoral and creative ways of dealing with
> all these situations.
>
> Synod of Bishops, Province of Southern Africa, 1997[4]

The South African bishops have not reached any consensus
on what this means for homosexuals. The 1997 report of
their Theological Commission[5] said that if the Church
should come to agree that homosexual love may be a
channel of God's grace, then such partnerships should be

blessed and such people ordained. Archbishop Desmond Tutu has been much more outspoken on their behalf:

> We reject them, treat them as pariahs, and push them outside of the confines of our church communities, and thereby we negate the consequences of their baptism and ours. We make them doubt that they are the children of God, and this must nearly be the ultimate blasphemy.[6]

His successor, Njongonkulu Ndungane, has also criticised the Lambeth resolution for ignoring the cultural context of the Bible and not listening to the experience of gay and lesbian people today.[7]

South Africa is, however, the exception. In most other African countries there is the most virulent opposition to homosexuality. President Robert Mugabe of Zimbabwe has said that 'Homosexuals are lower than dogs'. Ugandan president Yoweri Museveni announced in September 1999 a nationwide sweep for gays, following a media frenzy about two men getting married: 'I have told [the police] to look for homosexuals, lock them up and charge them . . . for their abominable acts. God created Adam and Eve. I did not see God creating man and man.'

In the summer after the Lambeth Conference I visited Uganda, whose Archbishop has been outspoken in support of the resolution and in criticism of the way that many American bishops have ignored or rejected it. 'They have turned their back' he told me, 'on the Gospel the missionaries brought to Africa. It is now our duty to uphold the truth.'

The claim that homosexuality is not part of African culture and was brought in by white culture is disputed within Africa itself.[8] It is, however, as now understood in the so-called First World, an expression of a more individu-alistic culture, which is very different from the customs and acts, including sexual acts, which gave meaning and stab-ility within traditional African society. Many of these persist, including polygamy. Indeed there are signs that, faced with the social and economic turmoil with which many African countries seem beset, there is some fallback to these traditional sources of identity and security through kinship.[9]

This can be seen in the pressure for new Anglican dio-ceses, and their bishops, to correspond with the older ethnic identities. It can also be seen in the perpetuation of a more patriarchal understanding of society, which – as we shall see in later chapters – is least likely to accommodate homo-sexuality. This will also impede the full participation of women, which will be a tragedy not only for them but also for society as a whole: on the evidence of our visit, it is the women who do more of the work, who have a deeper understanding of what is needed, and who are the key to the future. When I asked South Africa's Archbishop Njongonkulu Ndungane about this, he saw it as both tra-ditional and colonial: most other African churches have remained patriarchal because they have modelled them-selves on Western authoritarianism rather than their own local struggle.

What is also clear is that many of the church leaders in Uganda lack the perspective which a broader theological training might bring. Those who are graduates are most likely to have been trained at what is now the Christian University of Mukono. While there I asked what kind of theology they taught, and could find no African on the staff who would openly question the literal truth of a six-day creation, with Adam and Eve as historical figures. Other clergy are trained at regional theological colleges: at one we visited, the biblical teaching was done by two newly qualified English primary school teachers on a year's voluntary work.

Such observations do of course lay one open to the criticism of colonialism. Those American bishops who dismissed the Africans at Lambeth as 'still living in superstition' were, to my mind, quite out of order. The Ugandans themselves will respond that they are only being faithful to what the missionaries first taught them and what the Holy Spirit confirmed in the great East African Revival. They will point out that, given the way some followers of Darwin have linked together monkeys and black people, it's hardly surprising that they prefer Creationism to Evolution. They will also cite their own history – how in the 1886 Namugongo Martyrdom, a group of young Christians were put to death because they would not submit to the sexual advances of the king (although in this case, having visited the shrine, I wonder if the homosexual motive has grown in significance with its political usefulness; the fact is that there have also been 'heterosexual' killings at Namugongo, following the attempt of Obote's troops to rape female students).

More significant, I believe, is that the priorities of the Ugandan Church lie elsewhere. Like the Pakistani Anglicans who spoke so virulently against gay people at the Lambeth Conference, Uganda faces an increasingly powerful Muslim presence ready to take advantage of criticising any 'moral liberalism'. There is also within Uganda, seemingly on every street corner in the urban areas, an influx of fundamentalist Christian churches and organisations, largely American-funded, against which the Anglicans must similarly defend themselves.

And Uganda is a country at war. I spent a week in the northern dioceses on the border with the Sudan. We laid flowers on the grave of the bishop's wife who had been killed by a landmine. We visited camp after camp where literally thousands of Ugandans are forced to live, away from their own villages and any chance of growing their own crops, reliant on a United Nations food delivery every two weeks. The Church is in these displacement camps. The priests are baptising those babies who live long enough for this to be done. In some of them the bishop had his own hut where he would come and stay and be with his people. It's hardly surprising that what is grasping the imagination of Anglicans in, say, California, means little here.

I would, however, make two more observations from the experience of visiting Uganda. The first is that we are all affected, for better or worse, by the culture in which we are set. African bishops, sometimes rightly, accuse more liberal Christians of being led by the world rather than by Scripture. However, towards the end of our visit to Uganda, there took place in Kampala, at Namirembe Cathedral, the wedding of the 'kabaka', the king of the central area of Buganda. The service, conducted by the Archbishop, included much traditional African ceremonial and also a 'sermon' by President Museveni. Less public, but known by most of those present, was that the king already had an illegitimate son by a Rwandan woman, and the night before the wedding he had undergone a tribal ritual in which he had 'married' a thirteen-year-old virgin. Again, this is not meant as an English, colonial comment – our own recent experience of royal marriages has hardly been flawless – it is just to point out that the tensions between Christianity and culture are not only a problem for the 'wayward' West.

A final observation from Uganda comes from an experience on the road to one of its remotest dioceses, Karamoja. Driving along the unmade track, somewhat fearful of the armed tribesmen known to be controlling that area (and who stopped and killed another Western traveller the very next day), we came across a group of almost naked Africans carrying pointed sticks and going hunting. And yet, if you raised your eyes above the trees, there on the hilltop was a huge satellite receiver dish. Africa is changing, and where will the Church be? For some Christians, being able to beam in American tele-evangelists is part of the global fundamentalist dream, but this new technology will also open up a world which may need a more sophisticated approach to faith.

North America

Those minority of American (ECUSA) bishops who had helped put together the Kuala Lumpur statement before Lambeth returned home after the Conference with renewed energy to resist the advance of liberalism within the Episcopal Church in the United States. Various steps have been taken; the most radical, and the most controversial even amongst the more conservative bishops, has been the consecration, in Singapore, of two American priests as bishops to look after ECUSA congregations who no longer accept their own Diocesan.

As in South Africa, gay liberation has been the natural successor of the civil rights movement. The greatest opposition has come from the more conservative southern states where the 'religious right' has its stronghold: Senator Jesse

Helms has called it 'deliberate, disgusting, revolting conduct' and many black Christians have resisted the attempt to connect it with their own struggles.

> Don't expect us and our children to approve of, promote or elevate sexual preference to civil rights status. What's next, civil rights status on the basis of prostitution and paedophilia?
>
>   Alveda King, niece of Martin Luther King Jnr[10]

However, the Episcopal Church has gone further than any other part of the Anglican Communion in recognising gay and lesbian people. The former Presiding Bishop included homosexuals when he talked of it being an inclusive church in which there could be 'no outcasts'.

> When I was bishop of Okinawa, I had a congregation of people who were Hansen disease patients – lepers. At my first confirmation as Bishop, I asked that they not use the white linen cloths to cover the tops of their heads as they had done in the past, so that I might touch the heads of those confirmands. I did so because Jesus taught me to touch the lepers. It is Jesus, not me, who said – there will be no outcasts.[11]

This commitment to inclusivity has led many dioceses to accept not only lay people but also priests living in gay and lesbian partnerships. The call for the church to publicly 'bless' such same-sex unions came back to the 2000 General Convention, but it again narrowly failed to find acceptance. According to one bishop: 'Every time the church blesses the marriage of a straight couple, without sanctioning the covenant of gay and lesbian couples, it

strengthens the heterosexism of this society and the domination of straight people.'[12]

Most outspoken of those favouring such moves has been
Jack Spong, until recently Bishop of Newark.

> We have blessed fields when crops were planted, houses
> when newly occupied, pets in honour of St Francis, and
> even the hounds at a Virginia fox hunt. We have blessed
> MX missiles called 'Peacemakers' and warships whose
> sole purpose was to kill and destroy, calling them, in at
> least one instance, Corpus Christi – the Body of Christ.
> Why would it occur to us to withhold our blessing from
> a human relationship that produces a more complete
> person in each of its partners, because of their life
> together?[13]

Bill Swing, Bishop of California, told me about his own
spiritual journey in coming to accept 'practising' gay and
lesbian people. He had arrived in San Francisco before the
AIDS epidemic, and saw at first hand the suffering of
the gay community and the mutual fear that often characterised relationships with the Church. It was through this
pastoral contact, and then, in the increasingly open culture
of his city, learning to appreciate the faith and ministry of
gay and lesbian lay people and priests, that Bishop Swing
came to accept same-sex partnerships and believe that it
could be right for the Church to bless them.

With a sidelong reference to the way that the conservative
right seeks to defend 'family values' against homosexuals,
he told me: 'It's a family thing. I want to ask a mother and
father, if you had two children, one gay, one straight, would
you love the gay one less? And then, when your gay son or
lesbian daughter grows up, starts dating, wants to settle

down into a relationship, wouldn't you want them to be able to give and receive as much love as you knew when you were that age?'

What standards of behaviour does he expect then? 'I have got rid of the "historic lie". When I meet a gay or lesbian ordinand, I expect them to tell me the truth about their sexuality. What I'm looking for is whether it's a *healthy* sexuality, whether the person's relationships are healthy.' He therefore allows homosexual couples to share the rectory, and to come to diocesan functions as 'partners'.

Such freedom is not given to heterosexual couples who are not married, because for them marriage is possible. The bishop says that if at some future point there were to be a 'level playing field', so that all couples could have their partnership 'officially' recognised by the Church, the same discipline should apply to everyone. I sensed, however, that the overall discipline is much more open than in, say, the Church of England, with allowances for people preparing for marriage, unmarried couples in wholesome relationships who do not cause offence to the local church, and of course a much more widescale acceptance of divorced and remarried clergy, sometimes for the second or even third time.

Another issue arises here with regard to how the Church deals with same-sex unions. Bishop Otis Charles, the first openly gay bishop in the Episcopal Church, formerly Bishop of Utah and now retired in the Diocese of California, wants to resist the easy equivalence with heterosexual marriage. Gay people, he told me, have not yet had time to work out what alternatives are the right ones, and in any case they need to lead that debate rather than just follow rules which have been made by a primarily heterosexist Church.

Bishop Charles therefore wants to avoid identifying inclusivity with assimilation. There needs to be a distinctive gay community within the Church, where they can address their own agenda and where younger gay and lesbian Christians can find space and role-models. Other Episcopalians seem happier with a more post-gay culture: a senior priest in an east coast diocese, himself in an open gay partnership, said to me, 'We're interested in growing churches and developing faith. We've done the gay thing. It's no longer important. Our energy is now elsewhere.'

Will the Episcopal Church survive the gay debate? Bishop Swing says, 'Of course it will. The central message of the Gospel is not sex, nor is it homosexuality. This is only one of the issues where the Church must discern the mind of Christ. Any church that lives or dies on the homosexual issues lacks perspective.'

The present Presiding Bishop is committed to holding the different sides together and helping the Anglican Communion to see that changes which would be 'evangelistic suicide' in some places – for example, in Pakistan, as their bishops said so forcefully at Lambeth – are needed in other places where the Church has to apply the good news of the Gospel in a very different culture. Above all he has urged openness.

Questions about sexual self-expression – and more particularly homosexuality – abroad in the churches these days, oblige us not simply to react but to reflect upon our own sexuality in relationship to ourselves, to God, and in our relationships with those around us . . . Perhaps a greater degree of awareness will allow us to see our sexuality in the fuller light of God's creative imagination, a gift to be wisely and gracefully expressed as a way in which God loves us and is calling us to love others in Christ's name.[14]

A final word from North America is to mention briefly the situation in Canada. There are the same kinds of strain between liberals and conservatives, although the danger of the Church splitting between them is not as great as it is in the United States. In 1995 their General Synod acted to 'affirm the presence and contributions of gay men and lesbians in the life of the church'. One diocese, New Westminster, has come close to officially blessing same-sex unions, but held back at the last minute. In Toronto, after a painful and damaging court case over an openly gay priest, there is now a much more pastoral and evolving situation, and the bishop heads an open dialogue between the two opposing pressure groups, 'Integrity' and 'Fidelity'.

England

Around the corner from Portsmouth Cathedral, where I used to work, there's a small monument marking the spot where George Villiers, Duke of Buckingham, was assassinated in 1628. The motives for his murder are lost in history, but it's well known that he was one of James I's many gay lovers. The king himself had no problem excusing his behaviour: 'Jesus Christ did the same . . . Christ had his son John, and I have my George.' At the same time he approved of the continuing prosecutions for buggery and in his book defending absolute monarchy, *Basilicon Doron*, listed 'sodomy' as a 'horrible crime'.[15]

Perhaps this story sums up the hypocrisy which has sur-

rounded homosexuality through much of English history.
Or perhaps it alerts us to the problem of knowing exactly
what people meant when describing, let alone taking part
in, certain same-sex behaviour. What are we to make, for
example, of Anselm, Archbishop of Canterbury in the
twelfth century? When, in 1102, he refused to publish
the edict of the Council of London which said that 'sodomy'
must now be confessed as a sin, how was that related to
the passionate letters he was writing to other men, and how
did this in turn relate to his vow of celibacy?

> Wherever you go my love follows you, and wherever I
> remain my desire embraces you . . . How could I forget
> you? . . . he who is imprinted in my heart like a seal on
> wax.[16]

We will return to this question of definition, and what is
meant in different cultures, in later chapters.

Sodomy remained a hanging offence until 1861, when it
was replaced by penal servitude, possibly for life. In 1895
Oscar Wilde was given two years' hard labour for 'the love
that dare not speak its name': in Reading Gaol he wrote
'De Profundis', and A. E. Housman wrote his own bitterly
sarcastic poem:

> Oh who is that young sinner with the handcuffs on his
>   wrists?
> And what has he been after that they groan and shake
>   their fists?
> And wherefore is he wearing such a conscience-stricken
>   air?
> Oh they're taking him to prison for the colour of his
>   hair.[17]

It's often said that the British have more problems with sexuality in general than many other societies. Other countries seem to have got it more into proportion: for example, the Dutch, who are much more explicit with their young people but have far fewer teenage pregnancies, or the Italians who somehow manage to have one of the lowest birth-rates in Europe while still publicly affirming what the Vatican says about birth control! We English, however, still reflect something of that Victorian world where in their drawing rooms people would cover the legs of the piano, while on the streets of London forty thousand prostitutes plied their trade, many of them children.[18]

It would therefore not be surprising if the English have a particular problem with regard to homosexuality. It can be seen in an 'Establishment' which has put up a great fight against having openly gay people in the armed forces, and in what goes on in its public schools. When the writer Simon Raven was asked why he had been expelled from Charterhouse, he replied, 'The usual thing'.[19]

The publication of the Wolfenden Committee Report in 1957 was a shock for both society generally, and the Church. It proposed decriminalising homosexual behaviour between consenting adults in private. 'One might as well condone the Devil and all his works' said Lord Montgomery of Alamein in the House of Lords debate, going on to suggest that the age of consent should be raised to eighty. (Much later, in 1998, Lord Russell warned his fellow peers against the tendency to legislate against things we don't like, quoting the 1531 'Act against buggery, Welshmen, vagabonds and misdemeanours'!)

According to Michael Ramsey's biographer, it was only when Wolfenden was published, that 'he realised with surprise that he had never till this moment thought about the subject'.[20] Since then, bishops in the House of Lords have been careful to distinguish between changing the law, where reducing *criminal* liability could be seen as a matter of civil rights, and any change in how the Church understood the underlying *moral* issue.

Subsequent archbishops have upheld what they believed to be traditional morality. Robert Runcie softened a little, saying that he saw homosexuality

> neither as a sin nor as a sickness, but as a handicap; a state in which people have to cope with limitations and hardships, in which the fulfilment of heterosexual love is denied ... We are learning to regard the handicapped not with pity but with deep respect and an awareness that often through their handicap they can obtain a degree of self-giving and compassion which is denied to those not similarly afflicted.[21]

The present archbishop is uncompromising on the principle: 'I do not find any justification, from the Bible or from the entire Christian tradition, for sexual activity outside marriage.'[22]

Yet other things have been going on. At the practical level, it's said that the Church has continued with what it has probably always done, in ordaining homosexuals on the basis of 'Don't ask, don't tell':

> A significant minority of the clergy of the Church of England are gay ... It is precisely their homosexuality that has drawn them to Christ and gives them the insight and sensitivity that the Church of England values in their ministry.[23]

According to one study, 15 per cent of Church of England clergy are homosexual, and suffer high levels of stress.[24] Most bishops would say that's a serious exaggeration, but who can tell? An American commentator has observed:

> There was an English bishop of a major city, now retired, who routinely opposed ordination of gays and lambasted gay liberation in the press and then reassured his gay clergy privately of his personal support. This enabled him to keep his inner-city churches staffed while also keeping his gay clergy on a short leash.[25]

Whatever the Church of England does in the field of ethics will be publicly criticised, either for failing to meet the real needs of contemporary society, or by those who accuse it of selling the past. 'At the beginning of the century the Established Church was against buggery and in favour of fox hunting. At the end of the century it's the other way round.'[26]

Bishops are especially caught between their responsibility to reinterpret what the Church stands for and the fear of media sensationalism, but sometimes retirement brings the freedom to speak more openly:

> 'Christlikeness' [is] a creative living out of the values, priorities and attitudes that marked his full humanity . . . Erotic love can and often does have the same beneficial effects in the life of same sex couples.[27]

Nevertheless there have been various attempts to find a way forward. First came the Gloucester Report (1979). The Working Party said that 'there are circumstances in which individuals may justifiably choose to enter into a homosexual relationship',[28] but the Board for Social Responsibility added its own 'Critical Observations' such as: 'It is an error to reduce ethics to an undefined emotively elastic principle of "love" – and then to treat all other rules . . . as binding only insofar as they derive from that principle.' Many in the General Synod debate also said that its ethics were 'situationist', a highly subjective approach to morality which would open the door to many other alternatives to marriage,[29] and no vote was taken.

Then there was the 1990 Osborne Report to the House of Bishops, never intended for publication but leaked enough for reference to be made to it here.

> We do not think it possible to deny that there are circumstances in which individuals may justifiably choose to enter into a homosexual relationship with the hope of enjoying a companionship and physical expression of sexual love similar to that which is to be found in marriage.

Where does the Church of England now stand? At a synodical level, in 1987 the Revd Tony Higton introduced a resolution in which, he says, 'The General Synod all but unanimously reaffirmed the traditional biblical view that homosexual genital acts are sinful, i.e. to be met by a call to repentance.'[30] He also believes that those who persist in homosexual practice should be barred from Holy Communion.

Also from the evangelical stable came the St Andrew's Day Statement in 1995. Again, it says that the Church can never confer legitimacy on any alternatives to marriage and singleness. It does, however, put great emphasis on not defining people by their sexual affections:

> There is no such thing as 'a homosexual' or 'a hetero-
> sexual': there are human beings, male and female, called
> to redeemed humanity in Christ, endowed with a
> complex variety of emotional potentialities and
> threatened by a complex variety of forms of alienation.[31]

The most significant document, however, is the statement
made by the House of Bishops in 1991.[32] Produced in
response to the previous (1988) Lambeth Conference's call
for 'a deep and dispassionate study of the question of homosexuality', it does not claim to be 'the last word' on the
subject, but it does indicate where the bishops now stand,
and what they will, and will not, stand for in the behaviour
of their people. So it affirms human sexuality as a blessing,
and God's love for all people, whatever their sexual
orientation; it condemns what is popularly known as homophobia; it commends the three states of marriage, singleness
and celibacy; it accepts, with some reluctance, that some
church members will be in same-sex relationships and
should not be excluded for that reason. What it cannot do
is to make such allowances for ordained people, because,
given their distinctive calling, this would be seen as 'placing
that way of life in all respects on a par with heterosexual
marriage as a reflection of God's purposes in creation'.

For nearly ten years the bishops have stood by this statement. They have resisted attempts to tighten or to loosen
the Church's discipline on the grounds that the Church as
a whole has not yet fully discussed what they have put
forward. Their statement also says that in matters of practice they would respect the integrity of their clergy and not,
normally, delve into the sex lives of their ordinands. This
too has helped them hold the ground. But for how long
can this can continue?

Postscript

This summary of what has been happening in the Anglican Communion should not be taken to suggest that we ignore the equally difficult and valuable developments in other parts of the Church. There will be an opportunity to look at the Roman Catholic Church in a subsequent chapter. We might just note here that the Presbyterian Church (USA) has been through a time of trial and discovery very similar to that of their Episcopalian colleagues.[33] The Quakers seem to have come through it all with characteristic equanimity – for example, from New Zealand:

> Every individual's journey through life is unique. Some will make this journey alone, others in loving relationships – maybe in marriage or other forms of commitment. We need to ponder our own choices and try to understand the choices of others. Love has many shapes and colours and is not finite. It can not be measured or defined in terms of sexual orientation.[34]

In England, it was the Society of Friends who made the first significant move in the 1960s.[35] Since then the Methodist Church has struggled with the issue[36] and not reached a final conclusion. The United Reformed Church has had similar problems: after a number of discussion documents[37] its 1998 General Assembly made it possible for a local church to call a new minister who was in a gay or lesbian relationship. The next Assembly withdrew this, but subsequent consultations around the Church show that there is still considerable divergence on the right way forward.

2

Scripture

This chapter may get rather heavy. It even has some Greek words in it, and, as you will know, when the preacher says 'We will understand this even better if we look at the original Greek', it's time to turn off! (You will probably do the same when the sermon begins 'I have twelve points'; but you should also watch out for the preacher who claims 'three points' and then after twenty minutes says, 'And secondly . . .'!)

We have looked at how some Anglican churches around the world are dealing with the issues of sexuality, and homosexuality in particular. We have seen how different cultural contexts affect the way that the Church reacts, and perhaps begun to see that this may cloud the good news of the Gospel or, conversely, may be very important in understanding how that good news is to find genuine expression in the situation where the Church finds itself planted.

But Christian truth can never be determined by cultural context. At the very least it emerges from the dialogue between that social context and all the ways in which God has been known in the past, in the belief that through this conversation we may hear God speaking to us in the present. Paramount in all of this is the way that God has spoken through the Bible, and how he makes himself known through our reading of the Bible today.

So it is time to turn to the statement, contained in the Lambeth Conference resolution, that homosexual behaviour is 'incompatible with Scripture'. In this chapter we concentrate on what Scripture says and how we are to understand it, leaving to the next chapter the more general question about how Scripture and the Tradition of the Church interact with each other.

Another example: usury

Before looking at the rather complex issues of sexuality, however, it may be helpful to demonstrate the task before us by looking first at another and, on the surface, a simpler issue – usury. Usury is defined as 'the taking of iniquitous or illegal interest on a loan: formerly, interest of any kind on money lent'.[1] So what does the Bible say about it? What was meant by usury then, and how do we understand it today?

One could well claim that usury is incompatible with Scripture. The Old Testament says quite clearly that lending money for interest is wrong, especially when the person needs the money to survive.

> If any of your kin fall into difficulty and become dependent on you, you shall support them; they shall live with you as though resident aliens. Do not take interest in advance or otherwise make a profit from them, but fear your God; let them live with you. You shall not lend them your money at interest taken in advance, or provide them food at a profit.[2]

The Gospels make no direct reference to usury as such, but from Jesus' teaching on forgiveness and his use of the image of debt in the parables, one may assume that if anything he reinforces its unacceptability. In the Early Church it was explicitly denounced by Ambrose, Augustine and Jerome. It remained an outlawed activity for all Christians until the Reformation. In the Middle Ages Jewish people were forced into it on the grounds that Leviticus did not forbid them lending money to non-Jews, although that didn't prevent the Church from condemning them for doing it, and on many occasions burning them at the stake for it as well.

And yet, today, we all do it. Not only do we lend money and demand interest on it, but we have to campaign for the poorest countries of the world not to be enslaved by interest payments on debts taken out by dictator governments to buy arms from countries like ours to oppress their own people. In the world of stocks and shares, it is now moral not only to profit from investment in companies (who, it could be argued, are meeting human need) but also, in the 'futures markets' and from currency speculation, to make money from money itself.

Is usury, then, still incompatible with Scripture? No doubt there are some Christians, living the simple lifestyle, who believe it is, and avoid it. But Sunday by Sunday we offer up in the collection money which has come from the investments and interest payments of our church members. Month by month I receive a salary cheque which comes partly from the financial dealings of the Church Commissioners, and I have not yet felt the moral scruples to return it!

What then shall we say about Scripture? We might say that the biblical passages need to be read in context; for example, that Leviticus is about a type of cultic purity which the New Testament abandoned. We might point to the different social context, suggesting that what made sense in an agrarian economy doesn't fit in with the economic structures of the twenty-first century. We might argue that the biblical writers themselves could not envisage what we mean by 'investments' today, and they would not condemn them as 'usury'. We might claim that what the Bible says more broadly about enjoying creation, building community, reaping the harvest, yet not forgetting the poor, is more important in shaping what we do today than particular passages setting out how that was to be done in a different culture.

What I hope we would not do is simply dismiss what Scripture says as so out-of-touch to where we are today as to be irrelevant. On usury, and on sexuality to which we now turn, the Bible remains central. We need to know what Scripture says, what the original writers meant, and how we are to receive it today. In this process all Christians, from fundamentalists to liberals, depend on the promise of Jesus:

'I still have many things to say to you, but you cannot bear them now. When the Spirit of truth comes, he will guide you into all the truth; for he will not speak on his own, but will speak whatever he hears, and he will declare to you the things that are to come.[3]

It is also good to be reminded by St Paul that for the moment we see only as 'in a mirror, dimly', and until we get the full picture, faith and hope are good guides, but the greatest gift is love.[4]

Genesis

We start with the first book of the Bible, but not with
the story of Sodom and Gomorrah in Genesis 19 (nor the
similar episode in Judges 19). Although this story has
featured in much of the Church's later teaching on homosexuality, most commentators now believe it has little or
nothing to do with it.[5] The wickedness being denounced
here is violence, and the violation of the sacred code of
hospitality. It's about gang rape, not same-sex love. No
other biblical reference to Sodom gives homosexuality as
the reason for its destruction. Even the reference in the
Epistle of Jude (v.7) is to sex with angels, not someone of
the same gender. The second-century (AD) Jewish writer
Josephus is the first to connect the fall of Sodom with
homosexuality.

The crucial passages in Genesis are at the beginning: the
story, or rather stories, of creation. Although, as we have
seen, some parts of the Church still believe in the Garden
of Eden, and that we have 'fallen' from this ideal world
which God first created, most Christians since Darwin
understand these 'myths' in the context of Evolution.
Indeed, in the biblical tradition itself they have never been
'history' as we understand it today, but stories which
explain how, in the purposes of God, things are as they
are.

In the first creation story (1:1–2:3) we read:

God created humankind in his image, in the image of
God he created them; male and female he created
them. God blessed them, and God said to them, 'Be
fruitful and multiply, and fill the earth'.[6]

What this tells us is that humanity and sexuality are part of God's good creation, the sexual differentiation between men and women is God-given, and having children is a blessing. Does it also mean that procreation, or at least heterosexual marriage, is to be the only morally acceptable expression of human sexuality? Some think it does: 'If God was in favour of homosexuality he would have created Adam and Steve.'[7] Others disagree. Seeing how different people interpret it I am reminded of the amusing but insightful comment of Tom Wright, Canon of Westminster Abbey, 'Let him who is without an agenda throw the first stone'!

The second story (Genesis 2:4–3:24) is a little different:

> The LORD God said, 'It is not good that the man should be alone; I will make him a helper as his partner' . . . So the LORD God caused a deep sleep to fall upon the man, and he slept; then he took one of his ribs and closed up its place with flesh. And the rib that the LORD God had taken from the man he made into a woman and brought her to the man. Then the man said, 'This at last is bone of my bones and flesh of my flesh; this one shall be called Woman, for out of Man this one was taken.' Therefore a man leaves his father and his mother and clings to his wife, and they become one flesh.[8]

The emphasis here is on companionship, equality and mutuality: the purpose of human sexuality is seen as the expression and enrichment of human relationships. If anything, the stress is not on their difference as man and woman but on their similarity as human.[9]

On the basis of these two stories the Jewish and Christian traditions have built their understanding of marriage. Central to this has been how 'after the Fall' procreation was necessary for any human future, and then essential for the people of Israel to survive and grow. Although it is important to recognise how the understanding of marriage has changed through this process, and what we have today is very different from, say, Solomon's domestic arrangements or even the still quite patriarchal teaching of St Paul, the central elements are there in Genesis: one of God's greatest blessings is the faithful, loving, permanent partnership of a man and a woman, and the fruit of that relationship in the gift of children.

The question for our present study is not only what the creation stories affirm, but what they may exclude. How far is 'heterosexual complementarity' the only expression of God's gifts of sexuality and companionship? Is the Lutheran theologian Wolfhart Pannenberg right, for example, to say that heterosexual marriage is 'the goal of our creation as sexual beings'? Karl Barth went further, stating that according to Genesis it is the complementarity of male and female which is in the image of God, and so full humanity can only be achieved through a relationship with a member of the opposite sex.[10]

This is strange, because if when these stories talk about differentiation and complementarity the defining aspect is gender, why is this applied only to sexual intercourse and not the other activities, like work, for which we are created? Equally worrying, if our creation as complementary beings is primarily expressed in heterosexual coupling, is the implication that celibacy and singleness are less than ideal, or even sinful.

A fundamental question here is what it means to be made in the image of God (1:27). The claim that this is directly linked to being 'male and female' is doubtful because that distinction already belongs to the other animals that God has previously created. Here, in the creation of humankind, is something different: it is to do with relationship, which Christians will want to link to our understanding of the Trinity (persons-in-community), and it is to do with companionship, as developed in the other creation story. It is also to do with the kind of world which God gives them the power to go on creating: so in the second story God gives Adam great independence and freedom, allowing him to name the rest of creation, but not (by eating of the tree of knowledge) to usurp the place of God as creator. All of this should be helping to illuminate how we understand sexuality today, both within and beyond marriage

Before we leave Genesis, a word – in parenthesis – about another passage, which has nothing to do with sexuality but might help us in the larger task of how we use Scripture. In chapter nine there is the story of how Noah got drunk and when 'the morning after' he learns that his youngest son had seen him naked, he curses him: 'Cursed be Canaan; lowest of slaves shall he be to his brothers.'[11]

It is a passage which has caused untold suffering to the Canaanites, and the Palestinian people today. In 1980, on a World Council of Churches visit to Lebanon, I was asked to preach for the Anglican congregation of Palestinian refugees in Beirut. They began Matins with the New Testament reading because for them the Old Testament stories which Christians have used through the centuries had no part to play – they were part of their oppression.

From the opposite angle, on a visit a few years later to Central America, in a *favela* where thousands of people lived off the rubbish tips on the edge of Mexico City, I shared in a Eucharist where they were eagerly reading the Book of Exodus as God's promise to them of liberation from oppression: 'I have observed the misery of my people who are in Egypt; I have heard their cry.'[12]

I was reminded on both occasions that the community which is reading Scripture may be as significant as the community from which Scripture comes.

Leviticus

The crucial passages are: 'You shall not lie with a male as with a woman; it is an abomination.' and 'If a man lies with a male as with a woman, both of them have committed an abomination; they shall be put to death; their blood is upon them.'[13]

This is part of a much larger Holiness Code which determined whether people were ritually pure enough to come before God. Amongst other people who were excluded are those with defective eyesight or crushed testicles and the physically disabled. Lepers and menstruating women were also not welcome.

Behind this code there is a belief in certain natural categories of creation, which we no longer observe, so that just as God divided land and sea, darkness and light, so other things must be kept separate, like milk and meat, wool and linen. In his commentary on Leviticus, Philip Budd[14] observes that the word for 'abomination' in 18:22 is not that used up to now in the book, but the one we find in Deuteronomy 14:3–8 and 22:5, where it is applied to the sanction to eat sheep but not pig, and against a man wearing the clothes of a woman. (I will remember this when, on my next parish visit, and wearing a full-length purple cassock, I am offered a ham sandwich!)

The word 'abomination' is also directly linked to idolatry. There was an urgent need for Israel to keep separate from the surrounding nations, especially those whose 'idolatry' was expressed in cultic practices of sexual activity, including male and female prostitution. More generally, throughout the Old Testament and in St Paul's writings there is the contrast between idolatry – the world we make for ourselves – and creation – living in God's world as those who recognise its creator.

The Holiness Code is particularly concerned with bodily emissions. Procreation was essential for the future of God's people, so all sexual activity needed to be directed to that purpose. Another commentary on Leviticus[15] points out that 18:22 is preceded by a reference to the pagan Molech, known for destroying the life of children: 'The concern is with the loss of the male seed in infertile activity. The concern is not with the morality of sexual activity but with the pragmatics of producing children.' It is for this reason, as Alan Brash points out,[16] that there is no reference here to relationships between women.

We might also note in passing that another bodily emission which concerns the Holiness Code is blood. Four times in Leviticus (e.g. 17:10–14) and three times in Deuteronomy, the eating of blood is absolutely forbidden. The first Christians, even when they made circumcision optional, could not bring themselves to countermand this commandment (Acts 15:29 and 21:25). Yet today the Church happily ignores it and may deserve the tongue-in-cheek reprimand: 'The Bible unquestionably condemns homosexuality in both Old and New Testaments, but it condemns the eating of black pudding even more vehemently.'[17]

How then are we to understand Leviticus? One response

is not to bother. When did you last hear it read in your church, let alone a sermon preached from it? What it describes as an abomination belongs to a society long gone and can be dismissed, just as we dismiss Oliver Cromwell's denunciation of the Christmas pudding as 'an abominable, idolatrous thing'!

Yet many of the concepts of purity in Leviticus are informed by substantial moral considerations, not least 'you shall love your neighbour as yourself',[18] and St Paul's list of vices in 1 Corinthians 6 shows that some still have credibility on these grounds.[19] The problem is distinguishing between cultic and moral laws. In which category do we put what Leviticus says about homosexuality, let alone its command that disobedient children should be stoned? Bill Countryman, in his classic study *Dirt, Greed and Sex*,[20] argues that the New Testament did away with any such concepts of purity. Whether or not what is being talked about here is anything akin to what we mean by homosexuality today, for him the moral aspect is about *how* sexuality, of whatever orientation, is being expressed. What matters now is purity of heart.

Again, before we leave the Old Testament as a whole, another word – in parenthesis – about some other passages which influence the sexuality debate. First there is the Song of Songs, an unashamed celebration of erotic love, and perhaps one of the most difficult lessons for a residentiary canon to read at Choral Evensong – with the choirboys, for once, hanging on to every word! Then there are the stories of passionate friendships – David and Jonathan, Ruth and Naomi. These may not be about homosexuality as we understand it today, but at the very least they point us to the God-given love between two people which can be found beyond the institution of marriage.

The Gospels

The fact that Jesus says nothing about homosexuality has been used in their arguments by those on both sides of the present debate. It is important to note, however, two things that he does say and do.

First, he defends marriage and strengthens it by protecting the woman within it. Jewish tradition had a very patriarchal understanding of the married relationship: marriage was related to the need to secure the handing on of lineage and goods, and the wife was in many ways part of that property arrangement. In taking away the right of men to divorce their wife for any reason – and the meaning of 'unchastity' in the exception which only the Gospel of Matthew allows is very unclear – he sought to reduce the vulnerability into which women had been placed.

On the other hand, he did not – most people assume – choose marriage for himself. Indeed, he calls on his disciples, or at least those who are to be his closest followers, to sit loose to such human institutions in order to concentrate more on the coming Kingdom.[21] Even more worrying, he suggests that married relationships will not survive into the world which is to come.[22]

Secondly, in every way, he championed those who were on the outside. Disregarding the Jewish purity systems which we have just described, he welcomed the excluded, especially through touch. How far the 'poor' he blessed and the 'sinners' whose parties he attended included people of different sexualities, we do not know. Again, to put the question in that way may be to impose contemporary understandings of sexuality on a quite different culture. What we do know is that in the testimony of many gay and lesbian people today, the inclusiveness of Jesus' ministry is contrasted with what they experience from many other Christians. Many also claim that he transcended the laws of the Old Testament by the new commandment to love one other as he has loved us.[23]

Paul

There are three passages in the Epistles which almost certainly refer to homosexuality – but what was Paul actually writing about? The Greek world in which he lived made little moral differentiation between sexual affections: what mattered more was the social aspect, so that a man was not made inferior by a woman or by a man of a lower class. It also knew all about pederasty, which took three forms: buying sex with young boy prostitutes; taking a specific boy as a long-term lover; and providing boy-slaves for male guests.

In his first letter to the Corinthians, Paul says:

Do you not know that wrongdoers will not inherit the kingdom of God? Do not be deceived! Fornicators, idolaters, adulterers, male prostitutes (*malakoi*), sodomites (*arsenokoita*), thieves, the greedy, drunkards, revilers, robbers – none of these will inherit the kingdom of God.[24]

And Paul, or more likely one of his early followers, writes in 1 Timothy:

Now we know that the law is good, if one uses it legitimately. This means understanding that the law is laid

down not for the innocent but for the lawless and disobedient, for the godless and sinful, for the unholy and
profane, for those who kill their father or mother, for
murderers, fornicators, sodomites (*arsenokoita*), slave
traders, liars, perjurers, and whatever else is contrary to
the sound teaching that conforms to the glorious gospel
of the blessed God, which he entrusted to me.[25]

For some, these two passages are a clear condemnation
of homosexual behaviour. Others have sought alternative
interpretations of the Greek words which are being used.
They suggest that '*malakoi*' refers to effeminate call-boys
who sold their services as prostitutes, or even that the word
means those 'lacking self-control' and not necessarily
homosexual at all.[26] The other word – *arsen* (male) *koites*
(bed or sexual intercourse) – is not found before Paul's use
of it here. The Early Church Fathers used it for 'male
prostitute', again not necessarily homosexual; but it may
also mean, transliterated from the Hebrew word for 'lying
with a male', those pederastic men who bought the services
of the *malakoi*.[27] Certainly contemporary literature on prostitution condemned both the buyer and the seller.

However, the most crucial New Testament passage is in
Paul's letter to the Romans:

For this reason God gave them up to degrading passions.
Their women exchanged natural intercourse for
unnatural, and in the same way also the men, giving up
natural intercourse with women, were consumed with
passion for one another. Men committed shameless acts
with men and received in their own persons the due
penalty for their error.[28]

Again, for some this is an open-and-shut case: 'The passage is a very clear condemnation of both homosexual practice and lesbianism.'[29] It is, says Richard Hayes, not about individuals who have chosen homosexual behaviour, for whatever reason, but one illustration among others of how human fallenness has distorted God's created order – not sins which provoke God's judgement but symptoms of man's rebellion against God.

> Scripture affirms repeatedly that . . . our sexual desires rightly find fulfilment within heterosexual marriage. Once in the fallen state . . . we are 'slaves to sin' which distorts our perceptions, overpowers our wills. Thus . . . it cannot be maintained that a homosexual orientation is morally neutral because it is involuntary.[30]

Others want to ask more questions about it. Given Paul's larger picture here of idolatry, is his concern with the kind of homosexual behaviour which went on in pagan temples? Or, when he talks of people 'exchanging' what they do, is he referring to heterosexuals who deliberately choose homosexual behaviour contrary, as it were, to their own nature? Is this, therefore, again a reference to pederasty, which was according to some scholars the main form of male homosexual behaviour openly and widely practised in the Hellenistic world at the time, and often in vile and abusive ways? Certainly Paul's phrase 'male lying with male' is used by Philo to describe pederasty, and 'that which is against nature' and the Greek word for 'shame' were regularly used in secular critiques of it.[31]

There are also some questions to be asked here about what Paul means by 'natural'. Does he mean that which was 'normal' in contemporary culture, or that which God intended from the beginning? Even if it's the latter, we have to remember that Paul sets other things in the context of creation – for example, men having short hair (1 Cor. 11:7) and women being silent in church (1 Tim. 2:12) – which would be quite unnatural in many of our churches today.

We also need to ask whether Paul had any concept of a homosexual orientation, or the possibility of faithful, loving same-sex relationships? Although there were more positive expressions of homosexual relationships around in Greek society, Michael Vasey says that Paul, as a cosmopolitan Jew, would have been more aware of the homosexuality which was bound up with idolatry, slavery and social dominance, and, like most Jews and Stoics, he denounced it as the pursuit of self-gratification.[32]

Other biblical scholars raise larger questions about this passage. They draw attention to its 'rhetorical' character. Addressed to Jews, possibly even borrowing from a previous Jewish source,[33] Paul rehearses their standard condemnation of the pagans so that he can then, in chapter two, turn the tables on them to show that they too have completely failed, before going on in the rest of the epistle to contrast this universality of sin and its consequences in the justice of God, which is wrath, with the justice of God which is, in Christ, mercy and salvation.

The question remains how, in this great exposure of human failure and divine judgement, Paul understood the inclusion of homosexual behaviour, given that it comes in a list which includes, on the one hand, murderers and God-haters, and on the other, gossips and recalcitrant children. Bill Countryman, as we saw above, makes the distinction between uncleanness and sinfulness: Paul is saying that while, because of their idolatry, God has visited on (heterosexual) Gentile culture the unclean practice of homosexuality, no one in the Roman Church would ever have thought that he would wish to apply the purity laws of Leviticus to Gentiles.

> Paul rejected physical purity as a prerequisite of salvation or of membership in the Christian community ... Real dirt consisted not of specific foods, or sexual acts or of leprosy or corpses, but of arrogance, greed and other sins of social oppression or disruption. If certain acts, such as adultery, were still 'unclean' in this new sense, it was for reasons quite different from the purity ethics in Leviticus. Greed, not physical contamination, rendered them so.[34]

Some will feel that Countryman goes too far in rejecting the kind of rules which governed the Old Testament People of God, and which are to be found in different ways through the teachings of St Paul. A more cautious approach comes from Lisa Sowle Cahill:

> Early Christianity does not reject exchange relations, purity observance, or the family as such. But it does challenge and even reverse criteria of inclusion and exclusion, and gauges all moral relations by their success in dislodging power elites and including 'the poor' ... We need today to replicate that radical social change, but not necessarily its concrete moral practices.[35]

Nevertheless, they both raise the central question: how does the New Testament People of God understand itself as released from a fallen creation, liberated from the law which could only bring failure and judgement, and called to live the new life of love – the new creation in Christ?

This leads us, finally, to acknowledge, as we did with the Old Testament, that there are many passages which, though making no direct reference to sexuality, are still crucial to the current debate. We have already seen that the scandal of Jesus' ministry was its 'inclusivity', and we can now follow that through into the life of the Early Church. One example, in the story of the Ethiopian eunuch,[36] is how those who had been rejected because they were sexually different were no longer to be excluded: the prophet Isaiah had promised this,[37] and now it was fulfilled in the baptism by Philip.

The major challenge arose when Gentiles started being attracted into the new community of Jesus' followers. It came to a head at the Council of Jerusalem[38] when they decided that circumcision should not be a requirement for these non-Jews. How did they feel able to make such a radical departure from what had previously marked off God's People, separating the clean from the unclean? 'It seemed good to the Holy Spirit and to us,' they said. They were, as Paul would later write, no longer subject to the written code of the law (which no one could keep completely anyway), but living in the life of the Spirit. It is this radical theology of inclusion – salvation not by keeping rules but through God's free gift of grace – which may be more important than all of the specific texts we have studied in this chapter.

Conclusion

What, then, can we say to the question: 'Is homosexual behaviour incompatible with Scripture?' We have seen something of the complexity of text and interpretation, and maybe the best we can do here, as in future chapters, is to suggest a continuum of possible answers.

1. Homosexuality as a whole is rejected by Scripture as sinful. The fact that its writers may not have appreciated any distinction between orientation and expression is immaterial. Whether it is an involuntary part of the fallenness of all human nature, or a deliberately chosen way of thinking and behaving, Scripture's only answer is the call to repentance. This was the view taken by certain bishops at Lambeth, who could see little moral difference between homosexuality, paedophilia and bestiality.[39]

2. Scripture may say nothing explicitly about homosexual orientation, but it's very clear that homosexual behaviour can never be acceptable. John Stott argues this very cogently in his book *Same Sex Partnerships*,[40] where he defends the 'prohibition' texts, but bases his main argument on the creation passages found in Genesis and quoted by Jesus: heterosexual monogamy is the norm given by God in creation, and anything else is incompatible with what God has ordained.

3. Homosexual behaviour is condemned by Scripture, but we have to manage the gap between the biblical world and our own. For example, in his book twenty years ago, Bishop Peter Coleman concluded: 'Taken together, St Paul's writings repudiate homosexual behaviour as a vice of the Gentiles in Romans, as a bar to the Kingdom in Corinthians, and as an offence to be repudiated by the moral law in 1 Timothy',[41] but he also then tried to set the issue in its different cultural contexts.

More recently, Walter Wink also accepts that the Bible

clearly takes a negative view of same-sex relations, but he points out that Christians do not always take its teaching on sexuality at face value: for example, we reject the practice, demanded by the Old Testament, and quoted by Jesus without criticism, that if a man dies childless his oldest brother should have sexual intercourse with his widow so as to continue his line. In particular, Wink claims that Paul had no understanding that some people were homosexual by nature, and that for them to attempt to have heterosexual relationships would be, by definition, 'unnatural'.[42]

4. Homosexual behaviour is not incompatible with Scripture. This is the argument of those who still take the Bible very seriously, but who see the New Testament passages as referring to pederasty, prostitution or heterosexual depravity (or a combination of all three) and not the kind of same-sex loving relationships which may or may not have been around then, but are certainly around today. Into this category we may also put those who see the New Testament making new distinctions between 'uncleanness' and 'sinfulness' – the kind of argument put forward by Bill Countryman, who makes a similar case with regard to the change from 'property' (and therefore 'patriarchy') in married and other relationships.[43]

5. 'Compatibility with Scripture' is not the only consideration. The former Presiding Bishop of the Episcopal Church of the USA has said:

As Anglicans we discern God's will through Scripture, tradition and reason. However, some have chosen to embrace biblical literalism instead of our Anglican tradition. History tells us that biblical literalism was used

to support both the practice of slavery and the deni-
gration of women. We have moved past slavery and we
are moving past the oppression of women. It is time
to move past using literalistic readings of the Bible to
create prejudices against our gay and lesbian brothers
and sisters. Biblical literalism may be someone's tradition, but it's not our tradition and it's time we came
home to our Anglican roots.[44]

These words also set the scene for our next chapter.

3

Tradition

Some people enjoy living in a rapidly changing world. Others hate it: as the lady said when Britain changed to decimal currency, 'Why didn't they wait until all the old people had gone'! The hymn writer who gave us 'Abide with me' identified change with decay, but the reality is that without change, we die.

We move from Scripture to tradition, not something static and fixed, but the experience of the Church as it has sought to embody and to share the good news of Jesus Christ in each age and every culture, through the presence and power of the Holy Spirit. We need to recognise, of course, that Scripture itself – the communities from which and to which the various books came, and the final decision as to which books would be in and which left out – is part of this tradition; and so is the way that the role and authority of Scripture is understood in different parts of the Church.

Scripture in the Anglican tradition

Scripture has always occupied a central place in the Anglican tradition. It contains, according to the Thirty-nine

Articles, 'all things necessary to salvation'. The sixteenth-century reformers were anxious to do two things. One was to say that everything essential was there in Scripture, and so reject the Roman Catholic dependence on the teaching authority of the Church. The other was to distance themselves from the Puritans' claim that what Scripture said was self-evident and didn't need interpretation.

Richard Hooker, perhaps the most formative definer of Anglicanism, opposed the Puritan desire 'to enlarge the necessarie use of the word of God'. Scripture, he says, does frequently offer 'general axiomes, rules, and principles' of the 'lawe of reason', but by deduction from them persons are free to draw consequences not explicitly spelt out in Holy Writ. Hooker maintains that no one is obliged to 'deduce all his actions out of Scripture'; indeed, he says about some of the issues of church structure and worship which concerned the Church of his own time:

> truths there are, the verities of which time doth alter . . .
> Some new growne occasion always emerges, particularly
> in regard to doing, as opposed to believing: every man
> knoweth that the matter of faith is constant, the matter
> contrariwise of action daily changeable.[1]

The first of the four pillars of the 'Lambeth Quadrilateral' on which the Anglican Communion stands is therefore Scripture, spelt out by the 1888 Lambeth Conference as not only 'containing all things necessary for Salvation' but also as 'the rule and ultimate standard of faith'.[2] (The other three parts are Creeds, Sacraments and Ministry.) But Anglicans have also always believed that Scripture needs interpretation, and that's why the pursuit of Christian truth also requires tradition and reason, and within reason comes also experience. None of these things can stand alone.

So, in matters of sexuality, Anglicans would not accept, for example, priestly celibacy just because the tradition of the Church has held it to be necessary. Nor would they give overriding authority to experience: this would apply today to the experience of homosexual people, but also to the kind of claims made for 'spiritual experience'. The latter is interesting: historically, as their critics pointed out, the Puritans were not actually depending on Scripture alone but on their experience of what they believed God was directly saying to them through it. Something similar can be seen in many evangelical churches today with regard to divorce: there is a readiness to admit remarried people, because their situation is part of the lived experience and spiritual reality of the congregation, even though, as we shall see in a moment, it is contrary to at least an on-the-surface reading of Scripture.

Sadly, at the 1998 Lambeth Conference, this traditional emphasis on reading Scripture in context was not always taken seriously. One of the Conference consultants notes that in the resolutions from some of the African bishops:

> the underlying assumption is that the meaning of the scriptural message is self-evident and upheld in a uniform manner, and that the dialogue with the context of faith is one-way only: the Scripture changes cultures, but cultures must never intrude upon our use and authority of the text.[3]

Hence the too-easy use of the word 'incompatible' in the condemnation of homosexual behaviour. Hence, too, the Archbishop of Central Africa's need to defend himself

against some of the other bishops from 'the South' in one
Evensong sermon:

> I have resisted tyranny all my life and nor will I ever
> tolerate it from those who claim the love of the Bible
> over everyone else. Let not the intolerance of a variety
> of contexts inexorably lead us to intolerance, which, if
> unchecked, will find us with a band of vigilantes and
> fundamentalists . . . I pray to God that the spirit of Angli-
> canism will survive.[4]

It is, then, in the interplay between Scripture, tradition,
reason and experience that Anglicans seek to work faithfully
in the given context, rather than trying to impose one large,
all-encompassing picture. Michael Ramsey's definition of
Anglicanism was that it had this 'strikingly balanced witness
to Gospel and Church and sound learning', but he went
on to say that its greater credentials:

> 'are its incompleteness, with the tension and the travail
> in its soul. It is clumsy and untidy, it baffles neatness and
> logic. For it is sent not to commend itself as 'the best
> type of Christianity', but by its very brokenness to point
> to that universal Church wherein all have died.[5]

An important part of this process must be that we can
change our mind, or, as the Rule of one of the Anglican
Religious Communities puts it, 'Faithfulness to tradition
does not mean mere perpetuation or copying of ways from
the past but a creative recovery of the past as a source of
inspiration and guidance in our faithfulness to God's future,
the coming reign of God.'[6]

A good example of this development within tradition is

the way Lambeth Conferences have dealt with another thorny issue: birth control.[7] In 1908 it favoured the prosecution of all who publicly and professionally assisted preventative methods. By 1930 it had come to believe that it may be justifiable for Christians to practise it, as long as they are driven by serious moral reasons and not just on the grounds of selfishness or luxury, a decision which the *Church Times* editorial described as 'an enormous concession to the spirit and perhaps the practice of the modern world which is by no means guided in its conduct by Christian faith. It certainly involves a startling departure from the traditional teaching of Catholic moralists'.[8] By 1958, contraception had become not only acceptable but could also be a direct expression of Christian discipleship:

> Sexual intercourse is not by any means the only language of earthly love, but it is, in its full and right use, the most revealing . . . it is giving and receiving in the unity of two free spirits which is in itself good . . . Therefore it is utterly wrong to say that . . . intercourse ought not to be engaged in except with the willing intention of children.[9]

Dealing with difficult issues like birth control, divorce, and now homosexuality, raises the question of what holds Anglicans together and how much difference, including cultural diversity, can be accommodated. Christianity as a whole has never enjoyed, or been limited by, that clear rootedness in one culture which has characterised most other world religions. In particular, Anglicanism, although it grew out of Englishness, is today expressed in many different cultures: for example, its worship throughout the world was once centred on the (English) Book of Common Prayer, but now it is now being 'inculturated' by, for example, traditional African music and symbols in a Uganda village, and high-tech 'new age' worship in California.

Anglicans therefore struggle with holding all this together. There is talk of 'subsidiarity' – addressing issues at the local level rather then resorting to a central source of authority – and 'reception' – dealing with new ideas by accepting that change happens at a different pace and in different ways according to local circumstances, although recognising the risk of this leading to 'impaired communion'.[10]

In many ways none of this is new. It has been happening through the history of the Church as Christians have struggled with matters of faith and practice. It is, therefore, in this light that we return to our main concern: what has the Church believed through the centuries about sexuality in general, and about homosexuality in particular?

Tradition and sexuality: St Paul

Whatever Paul may, or may not, have said about homosexuality, he was very clear about marriage. For example, in chapter seven of his first letter to the Corinthians, Paul deals with the statement: 'It is well for a man not to touch a woman.'[11] These are not his words (as St John Chrysostom wrongly thought) but something which was being said in the church at Corinth. His reply is that, given the imminent coming of the Kingdom, it is probably best to remain unmarried. However, for those lacking his own self-control, or whatever else kept him from being married, possibly linked to his 'thorn in the flesh', he is willing to advise marriage rather than being 'aflame with passion'.

Two questions from the Church of today, as we deal with issues around marriage, might also be addressed to St Paul. First, what is the nature of the married relationship? In a world where property and patriarchy held sway rather than notions of mutuality and romantic love, at times Paul can sound remarkably 'modern': here in 1 Corinthians[12] he talks about equal rights and responsibilities, and in the letter he (or possibly one of his followers) wrote to the Ephesians he compares the relationship of husband and wife to the mystery between Christ and his Church.[13] That of course cannot be a relationship of equals, and indeed this passage also speaks of a man's 'headship' over a woman: he must love his wife, but she must be subject to him.[14] Perhaps what we can say about St Paul is that while he inevitably writes out of his own cultural and theological context, within this there is an affirmation of human relationships, including their physical expression, and even an affirmation of women, which later Christians have often failed to acknowledge, both in reading him and in their own teaching.

We might also note that, given the prominence it was later accorded, nowhere does Paul say anything about procreation in connection with marriage. Nor, indeed, did Jesus. What the later Church did take from their practice and teaching was the value of celibacy, seemingly at variance with any claim that heterosexual marriage is the norm from creation against which everything else is substandard.

And what about that other question – the failure of a marriage – with which so many parts of the Church are struggling today? Like Jesus, Paul if anything restricts the possibility of divorce: the only thing he is willing to contemplate is separation, and then only when one of the partners has become a Christian and the other hasn't.[15] The concept of entering into a second marriage is, as they say, 'incompatible with Scripture'.

Tradition and sexuality: the Early Church

Paul was writing, out of a Jewish background, into a Greek or 'Hellenistic' world, and we need to say a little about that culture in order to understand how subsequent leaders of the Church developed its teaching on matters of sexuality. To generalise, the Greeks had a 'dualistic' understanding of human nature, distinguishing between the body and the soul. The former, mortality, referred to our embodied, fleshly, changeable existence, passionate rather than rational. Immortality wasn't about the duration or continuation of life, but about higher levels of being, associated with the gods, truth, beauty and, reason.

This kind of philosophy is often called Gnosticism. At its best, Greek culture reflects the search to express the higher 'virtues' in art and in relationships. For others it was an invitation to licence: 'Eat, drink and be merry, for tomorrow we die.' But for many – for example, the Stoics – it meant the rejection of passion and pleasure, and seeing sex as only for human reproduction. Indeed, the idea that procreation entrapped a soul in matter may have led some Greeks to favour homosexual acts simply because they were not procreative.[16]

In the Jewish tradition, on the other hand, the human being was seen as a whole person, body and soul together. Human life is a linear process, rather than a matter of different dimensions and the constant need to move into a higher one. Blessing is to be found in this life: apart from some shadowy idea of 'Sheol', Jews saw their future primarily through their own children, and when ideas of resurrection developed it was to do with complete bodies again.

So the first Christians resisted 'Gnostic' ideas of dualism. They denounced as heretics those who said that matter is evil (the Manicheans) or that Jesus, if he was God, could not have had a real human body (the Docetists). They did not separate themselves from the world or mortify the body. However, as time went on, they began more to embrace Greek ideas of the soul as the place where holiness and godliness were to be found. They claimed support from what Paul writes about the battle between 'the flesh' and 'the spirit'. Their early experiences of martyrdom reinforced this belief, and it was later to find institutional expression in monasticism and the celibate life.

There were of course some very positive aspects to all of this: in a culture where most sex was linked to hierarchy, domination and property, avoiding it could be a radical declaration of belief in God's new community. But in the tradition a belief developed that the human body, and human emotions, were contrary to the life of the spirit. Amongst the Early Fathers we see this in Clement of Alexandria: 'to be entirely free from passion is to be most like God who is impassable' and 'To have sex for any other purpose than to have children is to violate nature'. We see it in St Jerome who said of the widow Paula when she abandoned her family to become a desert hermit, 'She overcame her love for her children by her love for God'. Origen believed that 'Anyone who enters the sanctuary of the church after the conjugal act and his own pollution, presumptuously intending to receive the eucharistic bread ... dishonours and profanes that which is sacred'.

He went on to castrate himself in order to become more holy.

The figure on whom this move away from a more 'holistic' view of human nature is usually blamed is St Augustine. 'The man responsible for welding Christianity and hostility to sexual pleasure into a systematic whole . . . Like many neurotics, he divorced love from sex.'[17] In fact, Augustine writes movingly about human desire, in loving one's neighbour, and most of all in seeking to love God: 'I tasted you, and now I hunger and thirst for you. You touched me, and I am aflame with love of your peace.'[18]

However, he could see *sexual* desire only as a rebellion against the divine love. It was part of that 'inward lust for domination' which had caused the fall, resulting in the shameful state of not being able to control our bodies. For Augustine, its only excuse was the need for procreation: 'What friend of wisdom and holy joy is there who, being married, would not prefer, if that were possible, to pro-create his children without this passion?'[19]

It's not surprising that this approach to sexuality led to the practice of clerical celibacy, and later, when it became compulsory, the assumption that those who received the call to the priesthood would surely also receive the gift and calling to be celibate. This was by no means always the case, which is one of the reasons why the reformers did away with the practice.

Tradition and sexuality: the later centuries

Today most Christians would deny that Scripture sees sexual desire in itself as alienation from God, and indeed

Augustine later admitted that it could have been present in some form before the fall, but for many centuries the Church taught that gratifying the sexual urge was sinful, albeit then pardonable within marriage. This is illustrated by the most famous of the 'Schoolmen' – Thomas Aquinas – whose teaching is summarised by one commentator as: 'once having produced the maximal or optimal number of children, a parent cannot have non-generative intercourse without sin unless a refusal to do his or her conjugal duty might drive the other partner to commit adultery'.[20]

However, what we also see creeping in here is what the Anglican Prayer Book was later to include as 'a remedy against sin and to avoid fornication' – marriage as a way of dealing with those 'flames of passion' which worried St Paul. Even more significantly, Reformation thinkers began to give greater significance to what Cranmer called 'the mutual society, help, and comfort, that the one ought to have of the other'. So the Anglican divine, Jeremy Taylor, encouraged married couples to engage in sexual intercourse in order to 'lighten and ease the cares and sadnesses of household affairs, or to endear each other'.[21] This was rather contrary to the Puritanism caricatured by a later writer as 'the haunting fear that someone, somewhere, may be happy'.[22]

This more positive understanding of sexuality, or at least the sexual side of marriage, has continued. Even in the Roman Catholic tradition, which continues to demand that the possibility of procreation be kept open (so no contraception, although, strangely, the 'rhythm method' is allowed), John Paul II has said that marital sex is a sign of total self-giving: 'Sexuality . . . is by no means something purely biological, but concerns the innermost being of the human person as such'.[23]

Marriage itself is changing. Many of the reasons are social and economic. The state of marriage is summarised by one writer as moving:

- from choosing a working partner to finding a companion to share your life;
- from the production of children to happiness and intimacy;
- from the family as the primary work group to the family as a nurturing nest for the young;
- from the establishment of kinship relationships to a focus on individual spiritual needs.[24]

What has also been significant is the simple biological discovery that reproduction is a partnership: we no longer believe, as most Christian moralists did in the past, that the seed of new life is owned by the male and just planted in the female to grow. As a result, all kinds of patriarchal thinking are falling, and the Church has to face new questions about what it is to be male and what it is to be female.

Marriage is therefore one area where the teaching of the Church has developed through history – an evolving tradition. But what about the Church's teaching on homosexuality?

Tradition and sexuality: homosexuality

Those Early Church Fathers who mention homosexuality tend to cite the prohibition in Leviticus. When Augustine recalled a certain male friendship of the past he wanted to repent of the 'dirt of lust' and the 'blackness of desire' which had contaminated it. Soon after the Church become 'established' by the Emperor Constantine, laws were passed against homosexual acts, and by the sixth century the punishment was burning at the stake (hence, perhaps, the slang term 'faggots'). However, John Boswell argues that the overall picture was somewhat different: 'In fact sustained and effective oppression of those engaged in homosexual behaviour was not known in Europe until the thirteenth century, and was never common in the Byzantine East.' Indeed he claims that up till then there are examples of liturgies for same-sex unions,[25] although other scholars think he overestimates their significance.

The problem here, as we noted in an earlier chapter when considering St Anselm, is knowing exactly what is meant. How far, for example, does this letter from the Anglo-Saxon priest-poet Alcuin, written to a bishop, indicate what we would term a 'homosexual relationship' today?

I think of your love and friendship with such sweet memories, Reverend Bishop, that I long for that lovely time when I may be able to clutch the neck of your sweetness with the fingers of my desires . . . how would I sink into your embraces . . . how would I cover with tightly pressed lips, not only your eyes, ears and mouth, but also your every finger and your toes, not once but many a time.[26]

The Third Lateran Council, in 1179, condemned homosexual people along with money-lenders, heretics, Jews, Muslims and mercenaries. Aquinas declared it to be 'unnatural', and worse than rape because there was no possibility of conception. Dante saw it as a perversion of love for the same reason. The Inquisition tortured and killed vast numbers. Neither the Reformation nor the

Counter Reformation caused the official teaching to be changed. When they arrived in the New World, the Puritans proclaimed the death penalty for both sodomy and adultery.

In recent years the Roman Catholic Church, like most others, has condemned homophobia and adopted a more pastoral approach to gay and lesbian people. The late Cardinal Hume insisted:

> All are precious in the eyes of God. The love which one person can have for and receive from another is a gift from God. Nonetheless, God expects homosexual people, as he does heterosexual people, to keep his law and to work towards achieving a difficult ideal, even if this will only be achieved gradually.

It has, however, been somewhat ambivalent on the issue itself. In 1975 the Vatican seemed to accept that the homosexual orientation was morally neutral,[27] but the 1986 Letter to the Bishops of the Catholic Church on the Pastoral Care of Homosexual Persons described it as 'ordered towards an intrinsic moral evil', 'an objective disorder' and 'a disordered sexual inclination which is essentially self-indulgent'.[28] The 1994 Catholic Catechism says nothing about homosexual orientation; it condemns homosexual acts utterly, and although it calls for discrimination to be 'avoided', it carefully limits this to *unjust* discrimination.

The Church and sexuality today

In looking at the tradition of the Church, and its teaching through the ages on sexuality, including marriage and

homosexuality, it's no accident that most of the sources
that have been cited have been men. One of the crucial
elements in what is happening today, affecting not just
male/female relations but same-sex ones as well, is the slow
erosion of this patriarchal world.

The other important element in the Church's teaching,
affecting all aspects of sexuality, is the relationship between
the physical and the spiritual, body and soul, sexuality and
spirituality. We have seen that for much of its history, the
Church, from the early influence of Greek thought, has
approached sexuality as a spiritual struggle against the flesh.
There are signs today that this is changing, with a new
appreciation of the body and of people as 'embodied souls'.

We can see this in the report prepared for the Diocese of
Newark (USA) in the 1980s, which said that sexuality isn't
simply a matter of behaviour, but something that goes to
the heart of our identity as persons. Our self-understanding,
our experience of ourselves as male or female, our ways of
experiencing and relating to others, are all reflective of our
being as sexual persons. The report said that we do not *have*
bodies, we *are* bodies, and the doctrine of the Incarnation
reminds us that God comes to us and we know God in the
flesh. We come to know God through our experience of
other embodied selves.[29]

Rowan Williams, now Archbishop of Wales, explores
some of this in what he calls 'The Body's Grace':

The whole story of creation, incarnation, and our incorporation into the fellowship of Christ's body tells us that
God desires us, as if we were God, as if we were
that unconditional response to God's giving that God's
self makes in the life of the Trinity. We are created so
that we may be caught up in this, so that we may grow

into the wholehearted love of God by learning that God loves us as God loves God.[30]

In the same article he begins to apply this to the issue of homosexuality, linking to some of the things we have already noted with regard to Scripture and tradition:

In a church which accepts the legitimacy of contraception, the absolute condemnation of same-sex relations of intimacy must rely either on a fundamentalist deployment of a number of very ambiguous biblical texts, or on a problematic and nonscriptural theory about natural complementarity, applied narrowly and crudely to physical differentiation without regard to psychological structures.[31]

Conclusion

So let us attempt another continuum, with its unavoidable generalisations, this time on how the tradition has treated sexuality.

1. A holistic understanding of life, with sex and children as a blessing, and marriage as a gift (albeit practised in a very patriarchal society) was rooted for the Jewish people in God's good creation and, following the fall, in the covenant he made with them. This survived the entry of 'Wisdom' into Jewish thought because the contrast was made between her gift of 'connectedness' and the rationality characterised by the Greek idea of 'the Word' ('*Logos*').[32] When Christians talked about this 'Word' they

avoided any degradation of the body by saying that it 'became flesh'.

2. In the Greek world there was a more dualistic approach to life, in which progress towards a higher level of being is hindered by worldly passion. This strongly influenced the way that the Church interpreted what the New Testament meant by 'the flesh', leading to the exaltation of male celibacy, the restriction of sex in marriage to procreation, and reinforcing the inferior status of women.

3. From the Reformation onwards, there was a movement towards seeing sex as an integral and valuable part of the marriage relationship – leading to a greater emphasis on romantic love and mutuality, especially as other social and economic forces led the family to become more domestic and nuclear.[33]

4. Today, there is more openness about how Christians should understand 'the body', perhaps returning to a more holistic approach. It is part of a more open attitude to sexuality in society as a whole, but also raises concerns in the Church because society's new attitudes are seen to threaten established patterns of sexual activity, especially marriage.

4

Reason

God has given human beings the ability and the responsibility to read and interpret Scripture, to receive and assess what the tradition of the Church has taught, and, from within the created order, to explore new insights which come from the discoveries of science and the fruit of intellectual struggle. This chapter looks at how homosexuality has been and continues to be understood. In the next chapter we will look at that part of our God-given 'reason' which comes more from direct personal experience today.

Homosexuality throughout history

How have previous cultures understood homosexuality? We have seen that an important strand in Judaic/Christian thinking has been the creation myth of woman and man originally forming one physical unity (Genesis 1:27), and the way that this oneness is renewed in marriage. For some, this leaves no room for same-sex relations.

On the other hand, the Greeks, who followed Plato, believed that originally there were three complete human beings – man and man, woman and woman, man and woman – and that it was the latter which was the less natural and therefore inferior. We find in the Greek world those who exalted homosexuality (Plutarch tells of an elite unit of homosexual soldiers in Thebes known as 'lovers' battalion'), those who condemned homosexuals as effeminate (the Stoics), and, perhaps the most common view, those who believed that where sexual affection was concerned what mattered was not so much the gender of the other person but their social position. While some claimed that this led to the noblest of relationships, it also led to the worst kinds of abuse.

Although in some ways the Church took over from the Greeks the idea that the most exalted relationships were between men – Aristotle believed that women were incapable of true friendship – homosexuality itself was gradually outlawed. A law in 390 threatened homosexuals with death by fire. Albertus Magnus (1206–80) saw it as a burning frenzy that could be spread from one person to another, for which the cure was either exorcism or, if that failed, burning at the stake. The Holy Roman Emperor, King Charles V, prescribed the death penalty in 1532 (Constitutio Criminalis Carolina), as did Henry VIII in England in 1533. Generally speaking, the crime being talked about here is 'sodomy', often extended to include anal intercourse with a woman as well. In the British Empire people could be executed for sodomy up to 1860.

And yet, as we have seen, Christian leaders like Anselm and Alcuin were writing passionate letters to other men. Another example is St Aelred of Rievaulx, who wrote 'On Spiritual Friendship', seemingly extolling love between men as a reflection of God's love for humankind.[1] Would they recognise what they were doing as what today is meant by being 'gay'? We do not know where they drew the line between orientation and behaviour, but in any case it's important to remember that until quite recent times, although certain acts were publicly forbidden, people were not socially defined by their sexuality. We will return to this social identity of homosexuality in a moment.

There is much evidence throughout history of those who certainly would be described as 'gay' or 'lesbian' today. In his book *Facing Our Differences*, Alan Brash makes a list of those recorded as having engaged in same-sex relationships. It includes Richard the Lionheart, Leonardo da Vinci, Michelangelo, Francis Bacon, Christopher Marlowe, Erasmus, Dostoevsky, Tchaikovsky, Herman Melville, John Maynard Keynes, Walt Whitman, James I of England, Henry III of France, Lawrence of Arabia, Kaiser Wilhelm II, Queen Christina of Sweden, Virginia Woolf, Katherine Mansfield and Greta Garbo.[2]

Defining and measuring homosexuality

The word 'homosexual' didn't appear until 1869, first in the German language and then in English twenty years later. Its appearance marked a change from talking about things which some people did to talking about the way that certain people are. It also denoted how what had been seen as a sin or a crime could now be regarded more as an illness. Not that everyone saw it as pathology: Havelock Ellis said it was a normal variant of human behaviour, like left-handedness, and Freud, though admitting it was less than optimal, wrote in a letter of 1935 that it was 'nothing to be ashamed of, no vice, no degradation . . . no illness'.

Others disagreed. The Nazis put thousands of suspected homosexuals into concentration camps – it's estimated that up to fifteen thousand died there. Well into this century there were attempts to change homosexual people by means of castration, aversion therapy, and worse: 'We're going to help you get better,' says a doctor in a 1950s film about the US Navy, as a gay man is strapped to a hospital bed, and electrodes attached to his head.[3] It wasn't until 1974 that American psychiatrists removed it from their official list of pathological conditions.

A major contributor to changed attitudes was the research published in 1948 in the Kinsey Report,[4] which claimed that of the men interviewed 37 per cent had had some overt homosexual experience leading to orgasm, 25 per cent had had more than incidental homosexual experience, and 4 per cent had been exclusively homosexual throughout adulthood, with the observation that this latter figure would have been 'a much larger proportion if there were no social constraints'. Kinsey invented a scale, with exclusive heterosexuality at one end and exclusive homosexuality at the other. He also used as reference both overt sexual experience and psychic responses (fantasies, dreams, erotic arousal). On this basis he said that a little over 18 per cent of males, and slightly fewer females, had at least half of their sexual experiences with a member of the same sex. When he asked whether for a period of at least three years between the ages of 16 and 55 a person's sexual behaviour and fantasies had been exclusively homosexual, he came up with the figure of 10 per cent.

Kinsey's statistics have been hotly debated, on the basis of the people he sampled (including prison inmates) and the questions he asked. By contrast, for example, Masters and Johnson[5] limited their survey to overt sexual experience, and did not include psychological feelings. Two more-conservative Christian commentators, Stanton L. Jones and

Don E. Workman,[6] cite other studies which produce a much lower estimate: Hunt suggests that 2 to 3 per cent of men are exclusively or near-exclusively homosexual, while Bieber says it's as low as 1 to 2 per cent.[7]

Causes

According to the Lepchas in the Sikkim Himalayas, homosexuality is the result of eating the flesh of a castrated pig.[8] When Europeans began to identify it as a condition, they too began to search for a cause. Freud believed that every person is born with bisexual potential, but for unknown reasons becomes either homo- or hetero-sexual. He called homosexuals 'inverts' and said there were three kinds: the 'biological', who were exclusively homosexual; the 'amphigenic', meaning bisexual; and the 'contingent', whose condition owed more to environmental factors, and who therefore might be able to change. Freud saw the main cause as psychological, linking it to the Oedipal complex and narcissism; it was for this reason that his later followers labelled it a 'disorder', which he had never done.

Studies this century have taken either a psychological or a biological direction. For the former, the cause is seen to lie in the areas of environment and behaviour. This may be the influence of early erotic and other learning experiences, like a seduction or life at school. It may lie in some disturbance in the parent-child relationship: Elizabeth Moberly, who locates the 'cause' in the failure to identify properly with the parent of the same sex, proposes, as the 'cure', the deliberate cultivation of non-erotic friendships with members of one's own sex in adulthood.[9]

Those who favour a more biological explanation have gone into the fields of genetics, hormonal imbalances (post- but more likely pre-natal), brain structure, and even socio- biological theories to do with natural selection. There is no conclusive evidence, and the possibility of finding the 'gay gene' raises both hopes and fears: would it establish that homosexual people are 'normal' after all, or would it lead to attempted genetic engineering to remove it?

Various studies, like comparing identical and non-ident- ical twins, have been quoted by one side and dismissed by the other. It may be that a biological disposition and certain experiences of socialisation come together, or it may be that one repels the other.

> If any one factor was the cause of homosexuality, it would have been discovered long ago. It is the outcome of a complex interaction between individual needs and dispo- sitions on the one hand, and environmental pressures, constraints and opportunities on the other. And causes vary from person to person.[10]

As Warren Blumenfeld and Diane Raymond say, there is no compelling answer, but what difference would it make anyway? There is no 'one explanation' for heterosexuality either![11]

Social acceptance

Where previous studies might have talked in terms of patho- logy, a summary of present research is more likely to conclude:

No consistent differences have been found for psychological adjustment, the capacity to form and maintain an intimate relationship, the ability to be a good parent, the likelihood of victimising children or adults, or the ability to function in a group or organisation.[12]

In today's world, in large parts of 'the North', the homosexual condition and homosexual behaviour are being accepted as an equal part of an increasingly diverse culture. In America they have a date that marks the turning point: 27 June 1969, when the New York police raided the Stonewall Inn and the gay members inside refused to surrender. From that grew a movement, a change of public policy, and in most cities today a gay community which enjoys recognition and respect. Indeed, some now talk of a 'post-gay culture', in which having a same-sex partner is no more a matter of social identity than being in a heterosexual relationship or staying single.

In Europe, sexual orientation is increasingly claimed as a proper component of any code of civil rights or equal opportunities policy. In the Netherlands and in France there is already a same-sex alternative to civil marriage. In Britain the incorporation of the European Convention of Human Rights led to a successful action against discrimination in the armed forces. The Government has tried to remove the controversial 'Clause 28', forbidding the promotion of homosexuality in schools, though the churches had grave reservations about any alternative lifestyle being presented as an equal to heterosexual marriage.

All of this has led to a new awareness of 'homophobia' and action against it. It's actually not a good term, because it suggests a clinical pathology, while it's more a social phenomenon like racism. For this reason the term 'heterosexism' is being more widely used, to the chagrin of those who dismiss it as another sign of political correctness.

However, not everyone is happy with this increasing acceptance. We saw earlier how large parts of the world, including most of Africa, are dubious of the homosexual condition, let alone its expression. For many fundamentalist Christians it remains anathema: 'The sin of homosexuality is not one shameful sin among many; rather it is the sin that most fully works out and manifests sin's vileness – it is the nadir of the degradation of sin.'[13]

Whilst seeking to be open to changing circumstances, the British churches, as we've also seen, have great reservations, or at least great uncertainties, about the way society is going. So, for example, the Church of England bishops were not of one mind on lowering the age of consent for young gay men: was it a civil matter, where it might be right to decriminalise a vulnerable group, or a moral issue, on which the different ethical assessments of homosexual behaviour should be brought to bear? But what should these ethical assessments be?

Orientation and expression

In the light of the new 'scientific' evidence on homosexuality – the application of what we are calling 'reason' – much of the Christian response has focused on the distinction between orientation and expression. This has even happened in some of the most conservative circles[14] – talking of 'loving the sinner, hating the sin' – although few openly acknowledge that this comes from new knowledge rather than Scripture or tradition.

However, this belief that the person is morally responsible only for what they do, not for who they are, may be too easy a way out. It leaves open a very basic question about orientation: is it part of creation, or a result of the fall? If the latter, the homosexual becomes rather like the alcoholic, bearing in his or her body a tragic expression of generic human sinfulness – but at the same time surrendering to it would be sinful because the result would be destructive of that person and their community.

If, however, a person's orientation is God-given, the claim is made that it should be welcomed, and used: 'Only a sadistic God would create hundreds and thousands of humans to be inherently homosexual and then deny them the right to sexual intimacy'.[15] The issue then becomes how the gift can be used in a moral way:

Accepting Christ and becoming a new creation in the family of God doesn't change a left-handed person into a right-handed person, but a genuine salvation experience should certainly cause a person to want to use that favoured hand, whether left or right, to do good and not evil.[16]

The other problem with this relatively new distinction between orientation and expression is that it rings bells with that ancient body/soul dualism which we have noted earlier.

Sexuality under dualism ceases to be a celebration of God's grace and becomes instead the occasion of God's judgement . . . Dualism gives a spurious credibility to the notion of an orientation that can be uncoupled from bodily expression.[17]

In contrast to this, Jesus' teaching about life in the Kingdom of God was all about embodied existence. Writing about the 'Issues in Human Sexuality' report, which focused on this distinction, Elizabeth Stuart criticises the bishops for their ambivalent attitude to the body.[18] Can one make such a division in a person's sexuality – or indeed their spirituality – between who they are and what they do? Is what people 'do' sexually only a matter of certain acts, or rather much more a part of what is going on in their minds and emotions? Kate Hunt, writing as 'a lesbian ordinand',[19] thinks it's just dishonest:

> The church in general appears to have latched on to the idea of orientation and practice with a huge sigh of relief. At last the church authorities can claim to be tolerant of homosexuality, whilst in actuality continuing to foster homophobia.

Seeking redefinitions

Another way in which concerned Christians have tried to respond to the new situation is to redefine homosexuality itself: no longer a sin, no longer an illness, so what is it? Some have seen it as a disability, something that is lacking or at least different from what most other people have, which must be met by the same kind of compassion and openness to alternative ways of expression that one would offer, say, to a person who lacked the ability to walk or speak.

Another way in which concerned Christians have tried

to respond to the new evidence is with the concept of 'less than ideal' or 'falling short'. Whilst usually still maintaining that heterosexuality is the God-given norm, allowances are made for some homosexual behaviour on the basis either that this is a sinful world in which people must do the best they can, or that those who engage in it sincerely believe that for them this is the only way of living out God's way of love.

> While heterosexual marriage is the normative or ideal context for sexual acts for the Christian, it is possible to judge sexual acts in other contexts as non-ideal but objectively justifiable in the exceptional situation, including that of the person with a strong homosexual identity.[20]

It is on these kinds of grounds that the Church of England bishops' report could tolerate lay people living in faithful gay relationships. Clergy, however, they asserted, needed to continue to be a public witness to God's original intention in the created order.

More conservative Christian commentators are not willing to be so accommodating. Jones and Workman (referred to above) use material from the Bell and Weinberg studies on homosexual behaviour patterns, and the results of psychological studies, to claim that even if it was right to declassify it as a pathology, it should still be seen as 'developmental abnormality'.[21]

Jeffrey Satinover is another American theologian who says that although homosexuality may not be a true illness, 'it may be thought an illness in the spiritual sense of "soul sickness" innate to fallen human nature'. He says that the kinds of changes described in this chapter are based not on scientific advance but are 'really a reversion to ancient pagan practice supported by a modern restatement of gnostic moral relativism'.[22]

New questions

Alongside the debate on the causes of homosexuality, and how acceptable it should be as an alternative condition and lifestyle, a new set of questions has emerged. Much of the debate until recently was engaged on the basis that there was such a thing as 'homosexuality', a condition which, whatever its causes and however it might or might not be expressed, existed as a fact. Indeed, it was thought to be a major achievement of the debate that we could talk of it in these terms rather than as the voluntary disposition (and possibly behaviour) of sinful men and women.

The questions which have now arisen are about how far sexuality is socially constructed. It is sometimes called the argument between Essentialism and Constructionism. It was begun by the gay French philosopher, Michel Foucault, and continued by theorists like David Greenberg, who says that sexuality is not a given, static condition like being black or left-handed, but rather it is learned behaviour, produced and interpreted in different ways by different societies at different times.[23] A radical feminist expression of this would be Rosemary Ruether's claim that no one is born heterosexual, but socialised into it by patriarchy among other factors, adding that for some it fails to take![24] The phrase 'queer theology' (objectionable to some) relates closely to this belief that there is no 'essential' sexuality or even gender.[25]

I apologised at the start of this book that it would not do justice to the lesbian perspective within homosexuality and perhaps here is the place to remedy that a little. When the debate was primarily in 'essentialist' terms, it was largely a debate belonging to gay men. Indeed, one accusation was that they were simply competing for equal status with heterosexual men in a male-dominated world: an example of that in the life of the Church would be the number of gay people who are very patriarchal and often misogynist. Lesbianism has had different origins and aims, and amongst these have been a desire to find expressions of sexuality which redefine its nature and purpose, seeking alternatives to a patriarchal understanding of the world.

It would be true to say that for these reasons some lesbians have deliberately chosen same-sex relationships rather than a male partner. But generally speaking, for both sexes, the essentialist versus constructionist debate is not about individuals being free to choose their own sexuality, but about how the sexuality that each individual comes to discover within himself or herself is affected by what society generally is able to describe and willing to allow.

This is a complicated debate. It affects what we have already discussed about how different cultures assess homosexuality. It illuminates the connections we have seen in previous cultures – for example, between heterosexuality and procreation. It puts into a new perspective the heterosexual/homosexual scale which Kinsey proposed, and particularly any definition of bisexuality. It opens up a new discussion about the relationship between friendship and sexual intimacy, which we will take up in the next chapter.

What this debate does not do is to suggest that all homosexuality is a voluntary – and, some might say, therefore sinful – rejection of our proper natural state. It raises questions about every aspect of each sexuality, including heterosexuality. Perhaps Michael Vasey was right when he recognised the presence of both people with 'an emotional and affectionate preference for their own gender' as a constant in human culture, and also the different configurations and social functions of what he called 'different homosexualities'.[26]

Conclusion

To end this chapter here is another attempt at a continuum, this time on the understanding of homosexuality.

1. What might have been acceptable in Greek society was seen by the Church as a sin, and as Christianity became the established religion of Europe, 'sodomy' became a criminal offence.

2. When scientific discovery began to establish the existence of a homosexual condition, it was first seen as something pathological – a psychological illness, calling for treatment and/or control.

3. Increased toleration of homosexual practice gradually led to some, mainly 'Northern', cultures accepting homosexual people as an alternative sub-culture, and in some cases even acting to remedy discrimination against them.

4. Faced with this new situation, Christians have tried to distinguish between orientation and expression, and some have been open to ways of redefining homosexuality. This has displeased both more

conservative Christians and many gay and lesbian people, who complain of the Church treating them as 'objects'.

5. From the 1980s there has been a new debate on the nature of homosexuality, and indeed all sexualities. Are there fixed categories, like heterosexuals, bisexuals and homosexuals, which run through all cultures? Or is our understanding of who people are also determined by the way that different societies are able to talk about, and perhaps permit, different kinds of sexuality?

5

Experience

We have seen how through the ages the search for Christian truth has been not so much an appeal to Scripture, tradition and reason as three separate resources, but rather found in the dynamic interplay between them. The fourth resource is experience, sometimes seen as part of reason. It is separated out here partly to make explicit the lived reality of the Christian community in the overall process, but also because when it comes to sexuality we are dealing with something which touches some of the deepest parts of our human experience. In his book *Body Theology*, James Nelson urges us to move from 'theologies of sexuality' to a 'sexual theology' which asks: 'What does our experience as human sexual beings tell us about how we read the scripture, interpret the tradition, and attempt to live out the meaning of the gospel?'[1]

The first scene of this book was set in that section of the 1998 Lambeth Conference which refused to admit a group of gay and lesbian Christians who wanted to share their experience. The final resolution included a commitment to 'listen to the experience of homosexual persons'.[2] What, then, shall we see and hear?

Perception and reality

Some Christians would expect to find little that is good. Their picture of homosexual life, especially male gay culture, is made up of three things. First there is AIDS. Certainly this has had a profound effect, although as any visitor to Uganda knows, on a world scale it's much more a heterosexual disease than the 'gay plague'. One response from the churches has been to see AIDS as God punishing those who disobey his law. So, for example, Pat Buchanan, spokesman for the US Religious Right: 'The poor homosexuals – they declared war on nature, and now nature has taken its revenge in AIDS.' Even John Stott, while showing deep compassion for AIDS sufferers, and especially its 'innocent victims', sees it as God's judgement on permissive society.[3]

However, Christians have also responded to the AIDS crisis by a variety of programmes from which have come not only fresh approaches to pastoral care but also new insights into how the Church can be with people where they are, in all their diversity, their brokenness and their longing.[4] In a collection of reflections on what has been learnt, Kenneth Leech says that the experience has challenged the Church:

The persistence of idealist views of sexuality makes a Christian engagement with the realities of flesh and human passion more difficult . . . Christian spirituality is at its best materialistic, incarnational, a spirituality of the whole person in communion. It is never a static essence, always a movement . . . a liberating movement.[5]

The second element in the popular imagination is promiscuity, usually condemned, but also sometimes secretly envied as a freedom not available to most heterosexual people. This is a difficult one to handle and assess. It is true that, whatever a person's sexuality, once they step beyond the strict boundaries of marital monogamy, all kinds of sexual licence become more possible, however inexcusable, and can have tragic results. Some of the statistics for the number of partners had by certain gay men are frightening. On the other hand, one has to ask some questions. Is it actually true that gay men, generally, are more promiscuous than heterosexual men, especially those who are unmarried? What evidence is there that homosexuality in itself makes a person more likely to act irresponsibly than someone who is 'straight'? And how far are they led in that direction by the circumstances they are in? These include being defined by their sexual preference (gay bars, gay clubs, etc.) in a way that would never happen to heterosexuals, the clandestine life of 'closet' gays, and society's reluctance to give public support and recognition to those in more committed relationships.

The third thing that, sadly, often figures in people's picture of homosexuality is child abuse. It's clear from the number of recent court cases, some of which have involved church institutions, that work is urgently needed on protecting children from abuse by adults, men and women, whatever their sexuality. Enforced celibacy has not helped. There is, however, no evidence that in itself homosexuality leads to the abuse of children. 'Contrary to popular opinion, the child molester is a relatively young, heterosexual man who is neither insane, nor retarded, nor sexually frustrated.'[6] Further American research concluded: 'Those offenders who selected underage male victims either have always done so exclusively or have regressed from adult heterosexual relationships. There were no homosexual, adult-oriented offenders in our sample who turned to children.'[7]

What most people do not imagine when they think about gay and lesbian people is the kind of loneliness and alienation that many experience. The Oasis project in the Diocese of California says: 'One third of all young people in this country who commit suicide are gay or lesbian'. Eric Marcus tells the story of eighteen-year-old Bobby, writing in his diary: 'Why did you do this to me, God? Am I going to hell? I want to be good. I want to amount to something. If I had that, I would be happy. Life is so cruel and unfair.' A year and a half later he jumped off a highway overpass, and landed in the path of an eight-wheel truck.[8] In New Zealand, even at the height of the epidemic, more gay men were dying of suicide than of AIDS.[9]

Homophobia

The homophobia which many gay and lesbian people experience is not just from outside the Church. 'There is no God if homosexuals are allowed into heaven' read the poster carried by one protester outside an American cathedral where a gay Episcopalian was being ordained. When in 1998 Matthew Shepard, a twenty-one-year-old student at the University of Wyoming, was murdered by two men because he was gay – they beat him beyond recognition, then tied him to a fence to die in the freezing weather, in a killing reminiscent of what whites used to do to blacks – protesters were seen at his funeral carrying placards saying 'God hates all gays, so good riddance'.

James Nelson suggests that there are elements within the Christian tradition which feed such hostility to gay people. These elements include 'justification by works' and the need to prove one's manhood, deep fears of sexual pleasure and defining gay people only in these terms, the lack of erotic love and the envy of those who seem to enjoy it, and the fear of death linked to the fact that gay sex is not reproductive.[10]

In recent years almost all church statements on the subject have condemned homophobia, although often expressing a concern that this should not be interpreted as accepting homosexuality. For this reason, the final plenary of the Lambeth Conference replaced this term with 'the irrational fear of homosexuals'. In its 1986 statement, the Vatican, while deploring homophobia, said that such violent and irrational attacks would be likely to increase if homosexuality itself were condoned.[11]

Healing and change

A different experience which homosexuals have been offered by the Church has been the invitation to 'Healing'. Mario Bergner is Director of 'Redeemed Life', a ministry of pastoral care for the 'sexually broken'. He writes of being healed of his homosexuality, and how through the power of the Holy Spirit he was able to confront his alienation from women and the feminine within himself.[12] Many such groups exist, although the umbrella organisation Exodus International suffered an early setback when two of its founding members fell in love and had to leave.

Many pro-gay and secular sources are hostile to such programmes, and suspicious of their results. 'There is no evidence indicating that such treatments are effective.'[13] The Bell, Weinberg and Hammersmith studies of 'Sexual Preference' show that the greatest chance of changing a person's sexual orientation is with what they call 'dissatis-fied homosexuals', but it appears that many of these are bisexual, perhaps already married, and more susceptible to change because a degree of heterosexual interest is already present. More generally they found that 'exclusive homo-sexuality seemed to be something that was firmly established by the end of adolescence and relatively imper-vious to change or modification by outside influences'.

It would be fair to say that many of the church projects which used to focus on changing a person's sexuality or on direct spiritual healing are now more concerned with helping gay and lesbian Christians to accept their orien-tation and live with it. They understand this to mean embracing chastity, and carefully keeping away from the temptations of the gay sub-culture. They are particularly critical of pro-gay groups within the Church who they feel make this Christian witness even more difficult.

John McNeil, while agreeing with such evangelical groups that the challenge to the gay or lesbian Christian is to live out who they are 'in a way that is consonant with Christian values', nevertheless claims that: 'Empirical studies have shown that the vast majority of gay people who have attempted a celibate lifestyle end up acting out their sexual needs in promiscuous and self-destructive ways'.[14] This is put less dramatically by another American writer:

Sullivan

If homosexuality is overcome by a renunciation of homosexual emotional and sexual union . . . their renunciation
of such love is not guided toward some ulterior or greater
goal – as the celibacy of the religious orders is designed
to intensify their devotion to God. Rather, the loveless
homosexual destiny is precisely towards nothing, a
negation of human fulfilment.[15]

Gay Christians

The picture that many Christians have is changing. They
are aware of groups like the Lesbian and Gay Christian
Movement. They are meeting homosexual people, inside
and outside the church. They are discovering that there
may be members of their own family, or their church family,
who are lesbian or gay. They are hearing real stories from
actual experience. Some of these have been published – for
example, *Speaking for Ourselves* from the United Reformed
Church[16] and *The Other Way? Anglican Gay and Lesbian
Journeys*[17] offered to the Lambeth Conference by a Church
of England group called 'Changing Attitudes'. They point
out that 'honesty' comes just after 'homosexuality' in most
Dictionaries of Christian Ethics!

There is in these stories a great deal of pain. There is the
experience of alienation and rejection:

For countless gay and lesbian people the Bible has
brought death, not life. Many speak of the Bible as a 'six-
gun', a pistol loaded with six texts that are used as bullets
– Bible bullets – to kill lesbian and gay people in a

contest about whether they can be full members of the community of faith.[18]

In his 'Confessions of a gay ordinand', Nicholas Southey writes:

> I know . . . gay men who regard struggles with Christianity and the churches as irrelevant and meaningless, a pursuit indulged in only by neurotics and insecure individuals who vainly seek affirmation from institutions which hound and hate them, and who in the process deny the full expression of their gay identities.[19]

And Michael Vasey again: 'For gay people . . . the churches are likely to remain places of danger . . . They may find themselves, like Jesus, suffering "outside the gate".'[20]

Some have given up knocking on the door. The Lambeth Conference resolution resulted in a number of people leaving the Church of England, including some priests. One wrote to his bishop in a Midlands diocese:

> The call to love my partner and love my priesthood have each been essential to my sense of Christian vocation – my integrity . . . (but) whereas before I lived my life discreetly, it feels to me now that I live deceitfully. I can no longer tolerate fear, repression, and dishonesty. I have had enough.[21]

Many continue the struggle within the Church, but not without great difficulty. It's sad that Henri Nouwen, the Catholic priest whose books help so many people on their spiritual journey, could write powerfully about the need to integrate spirituality and sexuality,[22] and yet we learn from his biographer that he struggled throughout his life to deal with his own homosexuality.[23] Coming to terms with one's own sexuality is as important, if not more important, for those who have accepted the celibate life. An Anglican religious talks of the insights this can bring:

> The experience of being different, and of having to conceal that difference from almost everyone on pain of intolerable sanctions, has tended to make gay and lesbian people especially sensitive to the mystery of identity, the inevitability of masks, the oppressive nature of conventions and stereotypes.[24]

Cardinal Ratzinger appears rather less optimistic:

> Homosexual persons . . . who seek to follow the Lord . . . are called to enact the will of God in their life by joining whatever sufferings and difficulties they experience in virtue of their condition to the sacrifice of the Lord's Cross.[25]

However, in many of the stories emerging from the experience of gay and lesbian Christians there is also much that is positive.

> We have experienced a huge growth in our faith and understanding of God's love through our relationship . . . That compassion and love has led to a deeper understanding of our priesthood, which has in turn fed through into the worship and life of the church.[26]

Some urge fellow Christians to raise their horizons to what

God is doing outside the narrow confines which the Church has often put into place.

> In the first two temptations (in Matthew), the devil tempts Jesus to identify himself on the devil's terms . . . The story parallels our own. 'If you are a child of God' some Christians tell us, 'become heterosexual; with God you can overcome your human sexual limitations.' We are children of God.[27]

In particular, the experience of gay and lesbian people offers to the rest of the Church new and challenging possibilities in two areas: inclusivity and spirituality.

A new inclusivity

We have seen that Scripture, when it is not reduced to the famous 'prohibition texts', has important things to say in the present discussion about a new creation, a community into which everyone is invited, including, and especially, those who were on the outside because they were thought 'unclean'.

> It is often where Scripture seems to fix the way relationships must be and roles must be set – women subordinate to man, man to cut his hair and woman not to, woman not to speak out in the church, slaves to be subordinate to their masters and obey them in fear and trembling as they obey Christ – that the church has heard in the gospel and in the prophetic and liberating words of both the Old Testament and the New Testament a counter word

that does not fix people in roles and relationships and
does not let cultural and social mores in this regard
become final definitions of who and what are in the
church and the kingdom.[28]

Some people have only discovered this acceptance in gay-
only congregations, such as those of the Metropolitan Community Church. Others who have 'come out' in ordinary
congregations have forced the minister and people to ask
where their boundaries lie: examples are the rural parish
where a gay couple asked if one of them could be on the
list of lay assistants at Holy Communion, and an inner-city
church where two lesbian women brought a child for
baptism and wanted both their names on the certificate.

It is out of such direct, pastoral situations that Christian
people find themselves doing theology. Will they draw the
line at certain types of relationship, or will their criteria be
based on the way in which these relationships are lived out?
Will they dismiss the claim 'All you need is love' as a naive
leftover from the 1960s, and argue that what we now need
is to reassert traditional moral standards which exclude
active homosexuals? Or will they go along with the
American Bishop who wrote to his diocese:

Jesus made the calling to love one another as he loved us
his special commandment. The following of this commandment is, above all, the sign of our unity. Paul wrote
that all other virtues are worth nothing without love. St
John of the Cross advised that 'in the evening we shall
be judged by love'. Love, however, we know to be much
more than a feeling. For Christians it is a discipline, and
our sexuality, as all of life, must be converted to become

part of a committed, faithful and self-giving love which
can be wholly blessed of God.[29]

Love is, of course, a slippery word. The love of God cannot
be reduced, as one American writer puts it, to God giving
us intimate partners and sexual fulfilment: the Bible says
that God's love is seen in the Trinity, and in Christ, and
our own love is but a weak and pale shadow of it.[30] But as
another American theologian, Bill Countryman, argues,
love is at the centre of the good news we are called to
share: gay people feel called to the gospel, he says, not to
heterosexuality; and being open, being less concerned
about its own purity, can help the Church to be more
centred and more outward-looking. 'It is very hard to carry
on evangelism from behind fortress walls.'

A new spirituality

A common thread in much new spirituality, which is influenced by the experience of gay and lesbian people, is the
rediscovery of eros.

The love which is desire or eros and which lies at the
root of all human inquiry, art and knowledge, as well as
the desire to love and be loved by another human being,
is being rightly rehabilitated as a form of human love in
the image of the divine. In desiring us and our response
God's love is shown as a blend of agape and eros
together.[31]

Christian writers have often distinguished between 'libido', the self-centred seeking of sensation and release; 'eros', the passionate desire for union; 'philia', the friendship which knows tenderness and compassion; and 'agape', which is about self-giving and finally self-sacrifice. C.S. Lewis wrote about the 'four loves'.[32] The problem with this kind of categorisation is that it destroys the continuity of all loving, and, especially with regard to eros, 'the self-giving love of a passionate God is conceived of as having nothing in common with the self-giving of a passionate lover'.[33] But eros is there in the Bible from the beginning. The fall did not create eros; it only perverted it, producing what Karl Barth called a vacillation between evil eroticism, on the one hand, and an evil absence of eroticism, on the other. Barth saw the Song of Songs as an expanded commentary on Genesis 2:25, celebrating love's intensity, restraint, mutuality and permanence.

Despite their often negative views of women and marriage, many of the Early Church Fathers, and medieval churchmen like Thomas Aquinas, could still see human passion and desire as God-given, and an insight, even an avenue, into the nature of God himself. In early English spirituality it is certainly there in Julian of Norwich, as she knows Christ saying to her:

> It is I whom you love
> It is I in whom you delight
> It is I for whom you long
> It is I whom you desire[34]

And it's there, albeit subconsciously, in much evangelical and charismatic worship today, where many of the prayers and songs have unnerving echoes of intercourse and orgasm.

Rather than sublimate human desires and loving into an other-worldly spirituality which risks the kind of dualism we have seen before, people are exploring the connection between their sexual experience and their life of prayer and worship. 'Unless we can experience and speak of God's grace in and through our bodies, in and through our sensuous connectedness to all reality, we do not know God's presence and power.'[35] Some expressions of it will nevertheless come as a shock to many traditional Christians:

It is surely obvious to anyone who has received the gift of their lover's body in love-making and the gift of Christ's body in the Eucharist that there are many unexplored parallels between these two life-sustaining, life-enhancing, life-creating activities.[36]

In Britain, this relationship has been particularly developed in the writings of Jim Cotter: 'Sexual energy is about the desire to be united with others (and within oneself and with God) and about the desire to create (both a new being and a new sense of being).'[37] In the United States, Chris Glazer has written a number of books on such themes, urging the rest of the Church to share in this rediscovery of sexuality as a way of experiencing God, as another form of sacrament.

From the majority heterosexual perspective, it is better to scapegoat, sacrifice and excommunicate those of us who are lesbian, gay, bisexual, and transgendered than for heterosexuals to confront their own alienation from their bodies and their sexuality, their own sexual infidelities and distortions, their own lack of spiritual-sexual integrity and certain gender identity, their own ignorance and injustice – in short, their own inability to recognise the sacramental nature of the body and of sexuality.[38]

Perhaps this is another point at which to repeat my apology that this book has been more about men than women. It's appropriate here because many of these new insights into spirituality come from feminist theologians. For example, Rebecca Parker writes: 'wherever passion, energy, joy, personal power and creativity emerge and converge, the experience can be felt as erotic'.[39] And these things, as she says, are the characteristics both of sexual intimacy and of God, particularly as seen in Jesus. There are pointers here as to how this more feminist definition of 'erotic' as 'pushing towards union' might express itself in a multitude of ways, and a question about whether gay men, perhaps responding to a homophobic and heterosexist society, have too easily identified it with genital, sexual activity.[40]

Lifestyles

Returning to more practical matters, what are the relation-ships and lifestyles which are emerging, and how should the Church be responding? This book has been primarily about same-sex relationships, but if only for the avoidance of doubt, we need to say something first about marriage. Nothing that may be said about alternatives to it can take away the fact that 'Lifelong marriage represents an unchanging ideal, and one which is the bedrock of a rapidly changing society'.[41]

Although not only, or necessarily, for the purpose of procreation, marriage remains for Christians the normative way of conceiving and bringing up children. Of course there are many stable and loving homes created by single parents and unmarried couples. Of course the ideal is not always achieved: marriages fail, and married life can also be the setting for abuse – physically, usually of women by men, and mentally, by either partner. But marriage remains the norm, not in the sense that anything else is inferior, but as the standard pattern, especially where children are involved.

Singleness and celibacy

An increasing number of people choose not to marry. In Britain today more than 6.5 million people live on their own, three times as many as 40 years ago,[42] and with a wide variety of lifestyle patterns. It is good that people no longer feel pressurised to marry, and particularly good if homosexual people do not feel forced into marriage. One estimate is that a quarter of gay men are married to women.[43] Those who attend support groups for gay and lesbian clergy remark on how many of them have been, or remain married, and the stress that this has put on both the partners.

It is important not to confuse singleness and celibacy. Those who remain single, whatever their sexual orientation, do so because this is their choice, or because the right person hasn't (yet) 'come along'. Celibates – some clergy, most members of religious communities, and a few others – believe that God has called them to a life where their sexuality is expressed not in sexual (i.e. genital) relationships but in a life of service to God and their neighbour. They are not 'angels', in the sense of being all spirit and no body, any more than Jesus was. They may be homosexual or heterosexual or anything in between. Like other single people they have a particular Christian witness in a culture which assumes that personal fulfilment must include physical sex.

Same-sex partnerships

In its 1998 resolution, the Lambeth Conference said that it 'cannot advise the legitimising or blessing of same-sex unions, nor the ordination of those involved in such unions'.[44] The reality, as we saw from North America, is that this is being increasingly questioned by parts of the Anglican Communion.[45] For example, a study document from Canada asks: having accepted that the orientation exists, whatever its cause, and that if such people were ever to form a sexually intimate human relationship it would have to be with a member of their own sex, 'they want to know why one set of norms and expectations for sexually committed, permanent, and covenanted relationships should not be the same for every Christian'.[46]

The American journalist Andrew Sullivan writes of such unions as the proper context for same-sex love. To those, both homosexual and heterosexual, who say that such unions cannot be accorded the same fundamental social recognition as marriage because homosexual love is somehow worth less, he argues that this is what used to said about inter-racial marriage.[47] He defends what he calls the 'conservative' case for gay marriage, in that, unlike the more flexible 'domestic partnership' agreements now allowed in some states, it would strengthen the traditional security of marriage in society as a whole.[48] It would also meet the criticism that there cannot be 'parity of esteem' because homosexual relationships are just a matter of individual agreement and not publicly acknowledged.

But should the Church bless such unions? One American bishop takes seriously the argument that

> many gay and lesbian couples already have, in their clandestine relationships, 'marriage by cohabitation', and that the church, to be true to its tradition, should invite such couples to come out of the closet and have their marriages publicly blessed.[49]

Other supporters say that for the Church to acknowledge such unions would enrich the understanding of heterosexual marriage, not least in showing men that there are alternatives to the kind of 'competitive masculinity' which they tend to bring to most relationships, including marriage. In Britain the case has been argued by Jeffrey John,[50] in direct opposition to those who would prefer the more open basis of friendship, which we will look at in a moment.

There are two major challenges here. The first one is to the Church where, as we have seen, a major concern has been the immorality of much homosexual behaviour. 'The much-proclaimed "committed, faithful homosexual relationships" are few and far between. Promiscuity is the norm in homosexual circles.'[51] Does the blessing of same-sex unions, whether or not they are equated with or likened to heterosexual marriage, provide a framework for encouraging behaviour and commitment more in line with what the Church has traditionally advocated? Those who can see no legitimacy whatsoever in the expression of homosexual love will of course find this a scandalous suggestion. Others

may be willing to consider it as a natural development of the
way that the Church has come to recognise the homosexual
orientation, and is increasingly finding amongst its own
members those who believe that this is a God-given state
which can find Christian expression in faithful, loving
relationships.

The second challenge is to homosexual people themselves. Firstly, what would be expected of those who seek
the Church's blessing on their union? Thomas E. Breidenthal, an American priest who sees same-sex unions as one
of the alternative 'Christian households' which the Church
should be encouraging, says that they should be marked by
the same discipline as the Church requires for all sexual
activity, whatever the orientation. It would need to be a
lifelong commitment, and exclusive of any other sexual
liaison. He does, however, observe: 'I suspect that urging
such disciplines on the church as a whole may prove more
controversial than blessing same-sex unions.'[52]

And then, what would be the implications for those who
do not seek such faithful, permanent relationships? Again,
for many Christians, it will be offensive even to ask the
question. There is marriage, and there is singleness or celibacy, and that's it. Some of those who now wish to add
same-sex unions as another option say that, if these were
to become a recognised part of the Church's life, that
should be the limit of all sexual (i.e. genital) activity. For
this reason many homosexuals are suspicious of 'gay marriage' – and some would add that it's a male-orientated,
patriarchal institution which they wouldn't want to support
anyway. So we are back at a major issue: what should be
the limits of any sexual activity? And we need to look at
that in the context of another significant development in
current thinking – the importance of friendship.

Friendship and sexuality

Friendship is an important part of the Christian tradition. We saw that the need for companionship was central to the second creation story in Genesis. Friendships are formed both within and beyond the family. As notions of family have changed, so has the extent of these other relationships. Michael Vasey probably overstates the point when he says,

> Christians before the 16th Century did not associate human desire primarily with the pursuit of heterosexual relationships and marital affection, and did not identify the home and the family as the prime context for friendship, intimacy and art[53]

but it's certainly true that the Church's idealisation of marriage has often placed too many expectations on those within it, and isolated those outside it.

We read in the Old Testament of the intense, passionate relationship between David and Jonathan so that David could say, mourning over his dead friend, 'I am distressed for you, my brother Jonathan; greatly beloved were you to me; your love to me was wonderful, passing the love of women.'[54] Some have seen something similar between Ruth and Naomi,[55] and between Jesus and John 'the disciple whom he loved'.[56] Were these relationships 'sexual'? Not if by that we mean 'genital', but they may have been in the sense of touching the deepest points of human longing to give oneself to another.

There is often some physical element in a deep friendship – embracing, even kissing. The question is whether there is any place, or justification, for anything more than that.

This is not to say that it's necessary – many of the deepest friendships, including people who share the same house and many parts of their lives, don't want it or need it. But what of those who do?

Elizabeth Stuart, in her book *Just Good Friends*,[57] offers a model of friendship which includes gay and lesbian partnerships, marriage, the experiences of celibates, and many others. The Church should be less hung up on what people 'do' and more concerned with how far these relationships reflect such (Christian) values as love, justice, mutual support, and even 'passionate vulnerability'.

> If we accept that there is no universal meaning to 'sex', but touch only takes on meaning in a context, that in a context of friendship, touching takes on the meaning of friendship, and that genital contact is not 'the ultimate' expression of closeness or affection, then the phenomenon of casual sex becomes less of a problem.[58]

Many traditional Christians will find this totally unacceptable: the only place for genital sex is in faithful, loving relationships, and, most would add, only those which the Church has blessed through marriage. However, many people outside the Church would be surprised that the questions are even being asked: as long as it's consensual, sex has ceased to be a forbidden activity, whether it's expressing a deep friendship or just for sensation and mutual self-gratification. In his controversial book *Godless Morality*, Richard Holloway doesn't mince his words: young people today see nothing wrong with 'shagging' for its own sake, and only if it leads on to sexual love does any code of faithfulness come into play.[59]

Holloway's case is that, as we try to redefine an ethic for

this new culture, we need to move away from moral systems and inherited authority codes, and stop claiming that they have been somehow God-given. Instead of this 'command morality', based often on fear, and often used against women and homosexuals, we need a new openness to experience, rational argument, acceptance of diversity, and above all seeking to love rather than to harm.

Again, many traditional Christians will find this very difficult. Apart from its challenge to Scripture and tradition, it raises yet again that difficult issue of 'dualism'. Sexual love is not just what people do with their bodies, it is how two people come together 'mind, body and soul'. It is the most profound way we know of being with another person in self-giving and self-realisation, in vulnerability and possession. That's why sexuality is sacred.

What then, finally, shall we say of homosexual love in this context? At the very least we need to hear the gay and lesbian Christians who believe that they truly experience this sacred love in their relationships one with another. Many struggle with relating this experience with what the Church is teaching, many are tempted by the free-for-all gay culture while searching for real partnership, but those who do find it believe that it is a gift from God.

Conclusion

My final 'continuum' comes from experience, the first-hand experience of Paul Wennes Egertson, a Lutheran bishop from southern California. In a moving article in Walter Wink's *Homosexuality and the Christian Faith* he tells what happened when the eldest of his six sons came home and told his parents that he was gay. He and his family had to ask themselves the kinds of questions we have been facing in this book. What were they to make of it? He says that they came up with the following possibilities:

1. It's a conscious and defiant rebellion against the laws of God – like prostitution – and so it deserves divine judgement.

2. It's an illness in which certain types of behaviour bring a bondage to addiction which can only be broken by total abstinence – like alcoholism – and so it requires celibacy.

3. It's a tragedy in nature – like infertility – and so it calls for compassion and whatever accommodation might be possible.

4. It's a variety in nature – like left-handedness – and so it's something to celebrate as a gift from God.

He concludes:

Since there are no experts who can answer these questions beyond the shadow of doubt, all we can do is digest the best information available from the testimony of gay and lesbian people, the ongoing results of scientific research, and the insights of serious biblical scholarship, praying that the Holy Spirit will lead us into all truth . . . As for me and my house, we're putting our money on the *celebration* line.[60]

6

Where Now?

Take your partners

If, like me, your teenage years included a youth club where it was thought that every young person should have at least some basic knowledge of what to do on the dance-floor, the call to 'Take your partners' was a moment of excitement and fear. Who would you find? Who would find you? People to look for. People to hide from. And of course that wanted yet dreaded experience of touching, holding another person. All the adventure and the terror of adolescent sexuality!

As we grow up, much of our life is made up of choosing which partners to embrace and which to avoid, in our work and public activity, and in our more private life of friend-ship and love. This book has been about the part that sexuality plays in these partnerships, and especially how Christian people deal with same-sex relationships. It's also been about a wider partnership – exploring the issue of homosexuality within the relationship between our contem-porary Church and those who have sought to follow Christ through the ages, and within the partnership between churches across the world today, especially in the Anglican Communion.

As we look to the future, we need to face the reality that gay and lesbian people are not going to go away. In Europe and North America they are more and more a visible part of everyday life, and they are part of the Church, however difficult that may be for some of its other members. They are becoming increasingly open, seeking what they believe to be their proper place within the People of God. We face a difficult and perhaps divisive period, and in the light of what we have explored in this book, I offer in this final chapter ten 'signposts' for moving ahead in a way which may help us to be more open to each other and to where God may be calling us, and which could also help us to stay together in the process.

Scripture

1. Be honest about our approach to Scripture

We need to admit that we all read Scripture selectively, and often we have our own agenda which determines what we take at face value and what we reinterpret or just gloss over. For example, even the most adamant interpreter of the creation stories as upholding heterosexual marriage does not despise singleness or celibacy. Despite what Leviticus says, few Christians today would want to see gay people put to death. Although Paul's list of depraved behaviour in Romans 1 includes, without distinction, greedy people and 'homosexuals', many Christians have no problem in seeing the first as 'just human nature' while denouncing the other as the worst of sins.

In times past the Church has taken what St Paul also says in Romans about earthly rulers[1] to defend the divine right of kings, whereas today we are more likely to find passages which point to democracy and human rights. At the height of the struggle to abolish slavery, both sides were able to find what they wanted in Scripture. Today, delegates to the Southern Baptist Convention are required to sign a declaration that their congregation does not condone homosexuality, but not that they will feed the hungry or visit those in prison, which, according to Jesus, are essential for entering the Kingdom of God.[2]

Some of the time we can argue that we are allowing Scripture to interpret itself from within Scripture. Much of the time we choose what meets our agenda, copes with our fears, and makes our life easier even if it adds to the burden of others.

2. Be consistent in our use of Scripture

In the Church of England debate on the ordination of women, the conservative evangelical opponents who said that this would be 'the thin end of the wedge' were in their way quite right. St Paul's teaching is clear, not only on the general point of male headship, but in the specific prohibition of women teaching or speaking in church, and for him this is deeply rooted in creation. And yet we went ahead. We cannot justify it on the grounds that Paul was talking about something different: two thousand years later the concepts of 'woman', 'church' and 'teaching/speaking' are the same. However, with regard to homosexuality, today we may be talking about something quite different from whatever Paul was describing: we now understand that it's part of a natural orientation, and that it can lead to faithful, loving relationships. Moreover, unlike what he says about women, Paul does not root what he says about homosexuality in any fundamental Christian doctrine. Why, then, has the Church felt able to depart from Scripture in one area, but refuses to re-examine the other on the grounds of 'incompatibility'?

Another significant inconsistency is the issue of divorce and remarriage. We have seen how the New Testament strengthened marriage, and made it more difficult for men to divorce their wives, thereby reducing the vulnerability of the woman. Jesus grounded this in creation, and Paul saw it sanctified in the almost parallel relationship between Christ and his Church. Why, then, are so many parts of the Church, including those who claim to be especially zealous in following Scripture, so willing to accept divorce, and to admit couples in a second marriage to receive Communion, and yet unable to see that there may be more to be said about homosexuality than an on-the-surface reading of Scripture may suggest?

The fact is that we cannot read Scripture apart from the context where we find ourselves today. Anglicans have always acknowledged this: since the Reformation we have believed that there will always be the need for such 'interpretation'. Of course this is a dangerous business: if we're not careful we will just use Scripture for our own purposes, and we will not hear it standing apart and judging us. Does that mean that we should be rejecting divorce and contraception, giving up our investments, and surrendering all our material goods so that we might have everything in common? Perhaps in all these areas, as with homosexuality, we are called to read Scripture in the same way that we try to lead the rest of our Christian lives, as adult people, aware of our sin, but also open to what the Holy Spirit is seeking to do among us.

Tradition

3. Be properly critical of what we have received from history

I put it as bluntly as that because, as we have seen, the Church's record on sexuality has not been its greatest glory. Early on, it departed from that more holistic view which shaped the Old Testament view of the human person, preferring the kind of body/soul dualism which denigrated the more sensual, erotic side of human experience and relationships, treated women as property or at best second class, and reduced even marriage to a second-best option. On the 'plus' side, it recognised the depth of (usually male) human longing, gave some protection to women, and, especially from the Reformation period onwards, laid the foundations for modern marriage.

So to be 'critical' is to acknowledge the mixed bag of our inheritance. It is to do what our predecessors did: to ask how, in our situation, we make sense of what we have received. And if new experience, new knowledge, leads us to different conclusions, it is in the tradition that we should be willing to develop and change.

4. Follow the processes as much as the conclusions

From the very beginning, Christianity has been a radical religion. The Pharisees saw this in Jesus and realised how dangerous it was. The first Christians at the Council of Jerusalem, as we have seen, were not afraid to do away with the most sacred things that separated Jew from Gentile, because they believed that God was doing something new among them. Indeed, as James tells them by quoting the prophets,[3] it was what they had received from the past that enabled them to make this response to their new situation, a response which could be both faithful and innovatory.

Writing to the Galatians, Paul rehearsed this in what may have been an early baptismal formula: the age-old distinctions between Jew and Greek, slave and free, male and female, have fallen away because of our new unity in Christ.[4] It is by no means self-evident that in our day he would have added 'gay and straight', but the main point is this: from its earliest days the Church was willing to depart from tradition, and to challenge inherited divisions, because of their belief in the radical inclusivity of the new creation in Christ. What does that say to us today?

Reason

5. *Take seriously what we now know*

There is a certain irony in self-proclaimed 'traditionalists' jetting across the world, and setting up Internet web-sites, in order to keep the Church in a pre-Enlightenment culture! While Christians do not believe that because something is modern it must be better, nor do we turn our back on new knowledge simply because it upsets some of the things we've believed before: when we tried that, with Galileo, with Darwin, and with countless others, it was the credibility of the Church which bore the final brunt.

The fact is that whatever the Early Church, or the medieval Church, understood by homosexuality, we now know two things which they probably didn't. First, we accept that it's the way that certain people are 'made' – it is, as we say, their 'orientation'. Few Christians, and no public statements from any of the major denominations, now doubt this. They may, as we have seen, draw from it very different conclusions. They may say that it's a disorder or a disability. Or – like more and more people in contemporary society – they may say that it's simply an alternative way, perhaps equivalent, perhaps second best, of being and relating to other persons.

Secondly, we can't escape the fact that there are, not least amongst us in the Church, men and women who have this orientation, and who in their relationships show the fruits of commitment, faithfulness and love. Many Christians will find it difficult to see these partnerships as being on a par with marriage, and perhaps one should recognise that they are rather different. Nevertheless, we can no longer pretend that there is 'marriage' and there is 'sodomy' – the world has moved on, and the Church needs to move on as well.

6. Be open to new understandings of sexuality

This takes us back to the final part of Chapter 5, and that complex debate about Essentialism and Constructionism: how far is our sexuality affected or determined by the culture we inhabit, and how far is homosexuality as we now know it a product of the kind of culture which, going back to the beginning of this book, is found in California but not in Uganda?

If we take this approach seriously, we find ourselves questioning our understanding of all sexualities, both homosexual and heterosexual. It forces us to look at how homosexuality is defined both by 'the gay lobby' and by a Church that brings to the table all the cultural inheritance, positive and negative, which we have been exploring in this book. Perhaps its greatest threat is not to homosexuals but to heterosexuals, even raising the question about whether what has been traditionally sidelined as 'bisexuality' is actually a more normative position. Perhaps for Christians the best response is what we saw in the St Andrew's Day Statement, and is mirrored in the Lambeth Conference resolution:

> There is no such thing as 'a homosexual' or 'a heterosexual': there are human beings, male and female, called to redeemed humanity in Christ, endowed with a complex variety of emotional potentialities and threatened by a complex variety of forms of alienation.[5]

Experience

7. Encourage loving, faithful relationships

However devalued the word may have become, Christians believe that God's first and last word is 'love'. However much it may have been romanticised out of all recognition for those who are trying to live it out in real relationships, it is love which is the beginning and the end of our seeking to share with one another what we experience in God's relationship with us.

Nothing must be allowed to weaken the Church's teaching that marriage is the God-given way for heterosexual couples to know and share this love, in a partnership which becomes much more than the sum of its parts, not least in the creation of a home where children are conceived and brought up. In addition to this, as we have seen, some parts of the Church seem ready to accept the loving, faithful partnerships of gay and lesbian couples, and even to bless some same-sex unions. Far from devaluing traditional teaching on marriage, they see this as reinforcing the idea of people committing themselves to each other in permanent relationships.

To suggest that this might be the way forward will scandalise many traditional Christians. To propose this as the only way forward will alarm many gay and lesbian people. But to reject any freeing-up of the present situation leaves the Church facing the question: what are we doing to people when we deny them the possibility of enriching, fulfilling relationships because, apparently through no fault of their own, they happen to have a different sexual orientation from the rest of us?

The report of the Church of England bishops, 'Issues in Human Sexuality', was, in a rather grudging way, willing to accept that for some lay people such expression of their homosexuality might be allowed. It drew the line with the clergy. Many gay and lesbian priests accept this teaching, and, even if they do not feel called to celibacy, find that their singleness contributes to their pastoral sensitivity and availability. Others do not, and we have to ask: is it right to impose celibacy on anyone, whatever their sexuality, and often in a way that prevents them discovering their sexuality? Equally, is it right to pressurise people, whatever their sexuality, into marriage? When the teaching of the Church, however well intentioned, leads to an unhealthy singleness or the pressure to get married, one has to ask what that does, not only to the priest himself or herself, but also to the people with whom they have to live and the people they are called to serve.

8. Look to the person, rather than the act

This is dangerous ground! If we're not careful we will fall back into that old dualism which says that what matters is not what you do with the body but what you mean by it, but we know that to be an artificial distinction because to be a person is to be body, mind and spirit together: the way we act with our bodies can't be separated from the rest of who we are, and in matters of sexuality it couldn't be closer.

Yet perhaps we've become too obsessed with sexuality in terms of what people physically 'do'. Perhaps in that sense we imitate too closely the culture in which we live, where the popular media is far more interested in who is doing what to whom, rather than the nature or depth of the relationship concerned. Perhaps, ironically, the Church has become rather like the 'gay culture' which seems more concerned with physical gratification rather than what two men, or two women, might actually mean to each other.

As we've seen, we need to rediscover friendship. Perhaps we drive people – homosexual, heterosexual, and those of an indeterminate sexuality – one way or another because there are so few openings for relationships which can be deep, even erotic, but still non-genital. Perhaps we should be more concerned with developing and encouraging relationships which reflect the affirming and self-giving love of Christ, and less worried about how these are expressed physically. Perhaps genuine intimacy is more important than genitalia.

Partnership in the Church

9. Living in solidarity and living with difference

We have moved out of a hierarchical world, in which those in power dictated what was normative for everyone else, and where divisions in the Church tended to arise from different hierarchies jockeying for power. We have moved into a much more individualistic world, more 'consumer-led' and with much greater diversity: in our day, division within the Church is more likely to arise from the tension between this way of being and the older hierarchical model.

There is much within our Christian faith which upholds the freedom of the individual, and much within our Christian history which has denied it. Yet we also need to confront the 'me' generation, the 'anything goes' culture. In the whole area of ethics we may have to accept that many of the old taken-for-granted values have gone – we live, in Alasdair MacIntyre's phrase, 'after virtue'[6] – but we play our part in this so-called post-modern world as those who are faithful to certain unnegotiable truths, not least the love of God at the centre of what makes sense of being a person and being in partnership with others.

For similar reasons, we cannot as Christians just give way to a 'you believe this, I believe that' approach to being together, or moving apart, in the Church. Nor even can we be content with the rather cheap model of 'reconciled diversity', meaning benign tolerance, which many Christians find an easier option to the costlier pursuit of real, 'visible', unity. We need to continue to struggle together for the truth, to find the right and godly balance between the call to solidarity and the recognition of difference. Nowhere is this more important – especially in the Anglican

Communion – than in the area of sexuality. As Archbishop Rowan Williams has written:

> Ours is a time when it is depressingly easy to make this or that issue a test of Christian orthodoxy . . . In other words the possibility is neglected that Christians beginning from the same premises and convictions may yet come to different conclusions about particular matters . . .
>
> It is really a matter of having a language in which to disagree rather than speaking two incompatible or mutually exclusive tongues.[7]

The last Lambeth Conference failed to meet this challenge. It will be the test of the next one whether it can hold together in a Christ-like unity those who have different understandings, in Christ, of where we should be going. If it can do so, it will be a witness not only to the wider Church as we seek that unity which is God's will and gift, but also to a wider world which desperately needs to learn how to live together, with difference, and yet in love.

The Partnership of the Trinity

10. *Take your partners with God!*

We are created to share in God's creative love. Part of this is through procreation – the gift of children – but that cannot be the sum of it. To be made in the image of God is to know something of that relatedness which is the Trinity – God who is known as a circular movement of love, a society, a *koinonia* of mutuality, transparency and co-equality. Elizabeth Stuart says: 'at the heart of God there is a dance of passionate friendship . . . Our just, passionate, mutual dances with each other reflect and are taken up into the dance of God'.[8]

It is not good for man, or woman, to be alone. When we 'take our partners' with those we love, we come close to that love which is at the centre of all things, the love for which we were created, the love for which Christ died.

Because God is Trinity, we understand the human being as becoming a person only in relationship: I become 'I' only in knowing and being known by another, and God is always the third person in the human trinity – the Source of love, the Incarnation of love, the Spirit which is love in and between us'.[9]

When I began this book, it was because I wanted to do what the 1998 Lambeth Conference manifestly failed to do – to look at human sexuality from within the proper context of Scripture, tradition and reason, within the Anglican Communion. I hope that what I've written helps with that process. But what I have discovered is that the real issue is about the nature of the Church – whether we are an inclusive or an exclusive community – and about the nature of God. For in the end it is a question of spirituality: we were created to love God and to love one another. Sex is only part of the way we know and express that love, and of course we live in a culture which often overemphasises the role it plays. But sex – human desire, loving intimacy, and, yes, physical intercourse – is an integral part of the way God gives to be together. The Church as a whole is not ready to embrace the possibility of this being found between people of the same sex. There is a lot of struggling with the truth to be done. But we cannot begin to do that unless we are willing to listen to each other, to pray together, and to seek to find in each other, and in the partnerships we enjoy, that love which takes us up into the dance of love which is at the heart of God.

Epilogue

Let me finish with three stories.

Peter is a priest in the north of England. I met him just once, at a conference, where late at night he told me his story – and like all the other stories in this book, names and some other details have been changed so that there is no way in which the person could be identified. Peter knew as a child that he was 'different'. He spent his adolescence praying that God would change him. He spent his college years trying to be heterosexual. He has spent the rest of his life giving the appearance that he has been called to celibacy when, in reality, it has been a mixture of loneliness and occasional lapses into sexual activity which have only added to his unhappiness. As a curate he nearly got engaged, and looking back he's grateful that at the last minute he ran away from what would have been a pretence. He is able to see that sublimating his desires and energies into priestly ministry has enabled him to give loving service to many people, and he is grateful for all that God has done through him. But deep in his heart there is still a longing for companionship, for intimacy, which the Church has never allowed him to explore in a public, healthy way. He dreads retirement, and the feeling of 'now it's too late'.

I met Stephen in an Episcopal parish in the USA where I had been preaching. He came into the vestry after the service, carrying Aaron, a three-year-old Afro-American boy. I'd seen him during Communion trying to encourage the reluctant toddler to come up for a blessing. 'Pat and I have been fostering him for a year now,' he said. 'He was baptised last month and we hope to adopt in the summer.' He had met Pat on the east coast, and on moving to their present diocese they had been able to have their union blessed by the parish priest. Pat is at the local seminary and hopes to be ordained next year, when the bishop will lay his hands on his head and say 'Send down the Holy Spirit upon your servant, Patrick, for the office and work of a priest in your Church'.

Jane first came to see me, some years before I became a bishop, because she was an ordinand and had been told to find a spiritual director. When I asked her whether she wanted to make her confession she said she couldn't because she didn't know what to confess. That's when she told me she was a lesbian, and asked whether or not it was a sin. As the months passed we tried to work through it all, but on the night before her selection conference she was on my doorstep in tears: how much should she tell them about who she really was? After many setbacks she was finally ordained, and after a month or two in her new parish she met Sarah, and fell in love. For the first time in her life, she said, she was able to be herself. But it was not easy – it never is between a priest and a member of the congregation, but in this case there also had to be all the secrecy and subterfuge. In the end, Sarah gave her an ultimatum: me or the Church. Jane refused to choose, and after another attempt to make it work, Sarah could take no more and left. It was Christmas, and after the morning service, Jane said she was going home to her parents, but in fact went back to her curate's flat. She was discovered next day, with a half-empty bottle of paracetamol lying beside her.

If anything, this book is for her.

Appendix 1

Report of the sub-section on Human Sexuality, and
commended to the Church by the final plenary,
Lambeth Conference 1998

Human sexuality is the gift of a loving God. It is a gift to be honoured and cherished by all people. As a means for the expression of the deepest human love and intimacy, sexuality has great power.

The Holy Scriptures and Christian tradition teach that human sexuality is intended by God to find its rightful and full expression between a man and a woman in the covenant of marriage, established by God in creation, and affirmed by our Lord Jesus Christ. Holy Matrimony is, by intention and divine purpose, to be a life-long, monogamous and unconditional commitment between a woman and a man. The Lambeth Conference 1978 and 1988 both affirmed 'marriage to be sacred, instituted by God and blessed by our Lord Jesus Christ'.

The New Testament and Christian history identify singleness and dedicated celibacy as Christ-like ways of living. The Church needs to recognise the demands and pressures upon both single and married people. Human beings define themselves by relationships with God and other persons. Churches need to find effective ways of encouraging Christ-like living, as well as providing opportunities for the flourishing of friendship, and the building of supportive community life.

We also recognise that there are among us persons who experience themselves as having a homosexual orientation. Many of these are members of the Church and are seeking the pastoral care, moral direction of the Church, and God's transforming power for the living of their lives and the ordering of relationships. We wish to assure them that they are loved by God and that all baptised, believing and faithful person, regardless of sexual orientation, are full members of the Body of Christ. We call upon the Church and all its members to work to end any discrimination on the basis of sexual orientation, and to oppose homophobia.

Clearly some expressions of sexuality are inherently contrary to the Christian way and are sinful. Such unacceptable expressions of sexuality include promiscuity, prostitution, incest, pornography, paedophilia, predatory sexual behaviour, and sadomasochism (all of which may be heterosexual and homosexual), adultery, violence against women and in families, rape and female circumcision. From a Christian perspective these forms of sexual expression remain sinful in any context. We are particularly concerned about the pressures on young people to engage in sexual activity at an early age, and we urge our Churches to teach the virtue of abstinence.

All human relationships need the transforming power of Christ which is available to all, and particularly when we fall short of biblical norms.

We must confess that we are not of one mind about homosexuality. Our variety of understanding encompasses:

1. those who believe that homosexual orientation is a

disorder, but that through the grace of Christ people can be changed, although not without pain and struggle.

2. those who believe that relationships between people of the same gender should not include genital expression, that this is the clear teaching of the Bible and of the Church universal, and that such activity (if unrepented of) is a barrier to the Kingdom of God.

3. those who believe that committed homosexual relationships fall short of the biblical norm, but are to be preferred to relationships that are anonymous and transient.

4. those who believe that the Church should accept and support or bless monogamous covenant relationships between homosexual people and that they may be ordained.

It appears that a majority of bishops is not prepared to bless same sex unions or to ordain active homosexuals. Furthermore many believe there should be a moratorium on such practices.

We have prayed, studied and discussed these issues, and we are unable to reach a common mind on the scriptural, theological, historical, and scientific questions that are raised. There is much that we do not yet understand. We request the Primates and the Anglican Consultative Council to establish a means of monitoring work done in the Communion on these issues and to share statements and resources among us.

The challenge to our Church is to maintain its unity while we seek, under the guidance of the Holy Spirit, to discern the way of Christ for the world today with respect to human sexuality. To do so will require sacrifice, trust, and charity towards one another, remembering that ulti-mately the identity of each person is defined in Christ.

There can be no description of human reality, in general or in particular, outside the reality of Christ. We must be on guard, therefore, against constructing any other ground for our identities than the redeemed humanity given us in him. Those who understand themselves as homosexuals, no more and no less than those who do not, are liable to false understandings based on personal or family histories, emotional dispositions, social settings and solidarities formed by common experiences or ambitions. Our sexual affections can no more define who we are than can our class, race or nationality. At the deepest ontological level, therefore, there is no such thing as 'a' homosexual or 'a' heterosexual; there are human beings, male and female, called to redeemed humanity in Christ, endowed with a complex variety of emotional potentialities and threatened by a complex variety of forms of alienation.

Appendix 2

Resolution 1.10 on Human Sexuality, agreed by the final plenary of the Lambeth Conference, 1998

This Conference:

- commends to the Church the sub-section report on human sexuality;
- in view of the teaching of Scripture, upholds faithfulness in marriage between a man and a woman in lifelong union, and believes that abstinence is right for those who are not called to marriage;
- recognises that there are among us persons who experience themselves as having a homosexual orientation. Many of these are members of the Church and are seeking the pastoral care, moral direction of the Church, and God's transforming power for the living of their lives and the ordering of relationships. We commit ourselves to listen to the experience of homosexual persons and we wish to assure them that they are loved by God and that all baptised, believing and faithful persons, regardless of sexual orientation, are full members of the Body of Christ;
- while rejecting homosexual practice as incompatible with Scripture, calls on all our people to minister pastorally and sensitively to all irrespective of sexual

orientation and to condemn irrational fear of homosexuals, violence within marriage and any trivialisation
and commercialisation of sex;

- cannot advise the legitimising or blessing of same
  sex unions nor ordaining those involved in same
  gender unions;
- requests the Primates and the ACC to establish a
  means of monitoring the work done on the subject
  of human sexuality in the Communion and to share
  statements and resources among us;
- notes the significance of the Kuala Lumpur Statement
  on Human Sexuality and the concerns expressed in
  resolutions IV.26, V.1, V.10, V.23 and V.35 on the
  authority of Scripture in matters of marriage and sexuality and asks the Primates and the ACC to include
  them in their monitoring process.

Notes

Introduction: Bishops in Conference

1   Official Report of the Lambeth Conference 1998 (Morehouse Publishing, 1999), p.93; reprinted in Appendix 1.
2   'Issues in Human Sexuality' (Church House Publishing, 1991).
3   Official Report of the Lambeth Conference 1998 (Morehouse Publishing, 1999), p.381; reprinted in Appendix 2.
4   Andrew Brown, 'Continental Rift', *Church Times*, September 1998.
5   Article in *Anglican Journal*, Anglican Church of Canada, December 1999.

Chapter 1: Around the Anglican Communion

1   Paul Farlam, 'Liberation through the law? The Constitution and the Church' in *Aliens in the Household of God*, ed. Paul Germond and Steve de Gruchy, (Cape Town & Johannesburg, David Philip, 1997).
2   André Muller, pastor in Reformeerde Kerk, in *Aliens in the Household of God*, op. cit.
3   Article by Robin Gill in *A Church for the 21st Century*, ed. Robert Hannaford (Gracewing, 1998).
4   Press statement issued by Provincial Press Office, 7 March 1997.
5   'Anglicans and Sexual Orientation', report by the Anglican Theological Commission, Church of the Province of Southern Africa, December 1997.

6 Foreword to *We were baptized too*. (SCM Press, 1996).

7 Lecture to the 'Healing Leaves' conference, Church Divinity School of the Pacific, Berkeley, California, January 2000.

8 Edward P. Antonio, 'Homosexuality and African Culture' in *Aliens in the Household of God*, op. cit.

9 Paul Gifford, *African Christianity – Its Public Role* (Hurst, 1998).

10 Quoted in *Sexuality and the Christian Body*, Eugene F. Rogers Jnr. (Blackwell, 1999).

11 Bishop Browning, former Presiding Bishop of the Episcopal Church of the USA, in his final address to the General Convention.

12 Rt Revd Charles E. Bennison, Jnr, Bishop of Pennsylvania, 1999.

13 John Shelby Spong, *Living in Sin* (Harper & Row, 1988).

14 Letter to the clergy of the US Episcopal Church from the Presiding Bishop, Autumn 1999.

15 Colin Spencer, *Homosexuality – A History* (Fourth Estate, 1995).

16 Letter of Anselm to Llanfrac, 'My beloved lover'.

17 Not published until after his death in 1936; *Collected Poems of A. E. Housman* (1939).

18 Warren J. Blumenfeld and Diane Raymond, *Looking at Gay and Lesbian Life* (Beacon Press, 1989).

19 Jeremy Paxman, *The English – a portrait of a people* (Michael Joseph, 1998).

20 Owen Chadwick, *Michael Ramsey: A Life* (Oxford University Press, 1990).

21 Margaret Duggan, *Runcie – The Making of an Archbishop* (Hodder & Stoughton, 1983).

22 Archbishop George Carey, address to Virginia Theological College, February 1997.

23 Michael Vasey, *Strangers and Friends* (Hodder & Stoughton, 1995).

24 Ben Fletcher, *Clergy under Stress* (Mowbray, 1990).

25   L. William Countryman, *Living on the Border of the Holy* (Morehouse, 1999).

26   Lord Onslow in *Have I got news for you*, BBC2, autumn 1999.

27   John Austin Baker, formerly Bishop of Salisbury, Lecture at St Martin-in-the-Fields, London, spring 1997.

28   *Homosexual Relationships: A Contribution to Discussion* (General Synod Board for Social Responsibility, 1979).

29   David Field, *New Dictionary of Christian Ethics and Pastoral Theology* (IVP, 1995).

30   Tony Higton, *Homosexuality and the Church* (ABWON, 1997).

31   Reproduced in *The Way Forward – Christian Voices on Homosexuality and the Church*, ed. Timothy Bradshaw (Hodder & Stoughton, 1997).

32   *Issues in Human Sexuality* (Church House Publishing, 1991).

33   See *Homosexuality in the Church*, ed. Jeffrey S. Siker (Westminster/John Knox Press, 1994), and *Homosexuality and Christian Community*, ed. Choon-Leong Seow (Westminster/John Knox Press, 1996).

34   Quaker Meeting, New Zealand, Statement of Affirmation and Reconciliation.

35   *Towards a Quaker View of Sex* (Society of Friends, 1963).

36   E.g. Report of the Commission on Human Sexuality (Methodist Publishing House, 1990).

37   E.g. *Homosexuality: A Christian View* (URC Church and Society Department, 1991).

Chapter 2: Scripture

1   *Chambers English Dictionary.*

2   Leviticus 25:35–37 NRSV.

3   Gospel of John 16:12 NRSV.

4   1 Corinthians 13.

5   D. S. Bailey, *Homosexuality and the Western Christian Tradition* (Harper & Row, 1955).

6   Genesis 1:27–28 NRSV.

7   Kenneth Meshoe, member of African Christian Democratic Party, speaking in SA Parliament, January 1995.

8   Genesis 2:18–24 NRSV.

9   Paul Germond, 'Heterosexism, homosexuality, and the Bible' in *Aliens in the Household of God*, op. cit.

10   *Church Dogmatics*, Vol. III pt 4, p.184.

11   Genesis 9:25 NRSV.

12   Exodus 3:7.

13   Leviticus 18:22 and 20:13.

14   Philip Budd, *New Century Bible Commentary* (Eerdmans, 1996).

15   Frank H. Gorman, *International Theological Commentary* (Eerdmans, 1997).

16   Alan A. Brash, *Facing our Differences* (World Council of Churches Publications, 1995).

17   David Bruce Taylor, *Homosexuality, the Bible and the Fundamentalist Tradition* (LGCM, 1999).

18   Leviticus 19:18 NRSV.

19   Thomas W. Gillespie in *Homosexuality and Christian Community*, ed. Choon-Leong Seow, op. cit.

20   L. William Countryman, *Dirt, Greed and Sex* (Fortress Press, 1988).

21   Matthew 10:37.

22   Luke 20:33–36.

23   John 13:34.

24   1 Corinthians 6:9 NRSV.

25   1 Timothy 1:9–10 NRSV.

26   James Boswell, *Christianity, Social Tolerance, and Homosexuality* (University of Chicago Press, 1980).

27   Robin Scroggs, *The New Testament and Homosexuality* (Philadelphia: Fortress Press, 1983).

28   Romans 1:26–27 NRSV.

29   Tony Higton, *What does the Bible say on homosexual practice?* (ABWON, 1997).
30   Richard B. Hayes in *Homosexuality in the Church*, ed. Jeffrey S. Siker, op. cit.
31   Scroggs, op. cit.
32   Vasey, *Strangers and Friends*, op. cit.
33   E. P. Saunders, *Paul, the Law, and the Jewish People* (1983).
34   Countryman, *Dirt, Greed and Sex*, op. cit.
35   Lisa Sowle Cahill, *Sex, Gender and Christian Ethics* (Cambridge University Press, 1996).
36   Acts 8:26–40.
37   Isaiah 56:2–8.
38   Acts 15:1–29.
39   Resolution from the West African Region to the Lambeth Conference 1998.
40   John Stott, *Same Sex Partnerships* (Marshall Pickering, 1998).
41   Peter Coleman, *Christian attitudes to Homosexuality* (SPCK, 1980).
42   Walter Wink (ed.), *Homosexuality and Christian Faith* (Fortress Press, 1999).
43   Countryman, *Dirt, Greed and Sex*, op. cit.
44   Bishop Browning, final address to the General Convention, 1997.

Chapter 3: Tradition

1   Quoted in John L. Kater, 'Faithful Church, Plural World: Diversity at Lambeth 1998', *Anglican Theological Review* LXXXI:2, 1999.
2   Alan Stephenson, *Anglicanism and the Lambeth Conferences*, (SPCK, 1978).
3   John L Kater, 'Faithful Church, Plural World: Diversity at Lambeth 1998', op. cit.
4   Khotso Makhulu, Archbishop of Central Africa, speaking at 1998 Lambeth Conference.

5 A. M. Ramsey, *The Gospel and the Catholic Church* (Longmans Green & Co., 1936).

6 Rule of Society of St John the Evangelist (1997).

7 See Stephenson, op. cit.

8 *Church Times*, 15 August 1930.

9 Report of the Lambeth Conference, 1958

10 'The Virginia Report' in the Official Report of the Lambeth Conference 1998 (Morehouse Publishing, 1999).

11 1 Corinthians 7:1.

12 1 Corinthians 7:3f.

13 Ephesians 5:25–33.

14 Ephesians 5:22–24.

15 1 Corinthians 7:15.

16 Spencer, *Homosexuality – A History*, op. cit.

17 Uta Ranke-Heineman, *Eunuchs for the Kingdom of Heaven – The Catholic Church and Sexuality* (Andre Deutsch, 1990).

18 *The Confessions of St Augustine*, Bk 10, ch. 27.

19 St Augustine, *City of God*, Book XIV, ch. 16 (Tr. J.W.C. Wand, Oxford University Press, 1963).

20 Ranke-Heineman, *Eunuchs for Heaven* op. cit.

21 Jeremy Taylor, 'The Rule and Exercise of Holy Living and Dying', quoted in Richard J. Foster, *'Money, Sex and Power'* (Harper & Row, 1985).

22 H. L. Mencken, quoted in Bill Bryson, *Notes from a Big Country* (Doubleday, 1998).

23 'Familias Consortio', quoted in Cahill, *Sex, Gender and Christian Ethics*, op. cit.

24 E. J. Graff, *What is Marriage for?* (Boston: Beacon Press, 1999).

25 John Boswell, *Same-Sex Unions in Premodern Europe* (New York: Villard Books, 1994).

26 Heinrich Fichtenau, *'The Carolingian Empire'* (University of Toronto Press, 1979).

27 'Declaration on Certain Questions concerning Sexual Ethics' Congregation for the Doctrine of Faith, 1975.

28   Congregation for the Doctrine of Faith, 1986.
29   Task Force on Changing Patterns of Sexuality and Family Life, Diocese of Newark, 1980s.
30   Rowan Williams, 'The Body's Grace' in *Our Selves, Our Souls and Bodies*, ed. Charles Hefling (Boston: Cowley Publications, 1996).
31   Ibid.
32   Mary Grey, *The Wisdom of Fools? Seeking Revelation for Today* (SPCK, 1993).
33   See *Something to Celebrate – Valuing Families in Church and Society* (Church House Publishing, 1995).

Chapter 4: Reason

1   Adrian Thatcher and Elizabeth Stuart, *Christian Perspectives on Sexuality and Gender* (Eerdmans, Gracewing, 1996).
2   Alan A. Brash, *Facing our Differences* (World Council of Churches Publications, 1995).
3   Chandler Burr in *Homosexuality in the Church*, ed. Jeffrey S. Siker (Westminster/John Knox Press, 1994).
4   A. C. Kinsey, W. B. Pomeroy and C. Martin, *Sexual Behaviour in the Human Male* (Philadelphia: W. B. Saunders, 1948).
5   W. H. Masters, V. E. Johnson, and R. C. Kolodny, *Human Sexuality* (Longman, 5th edn., 1995).
6   Stanton L. Jones and Don E. Workman in *Homosexuality in the Church*, op. cit.
7   Ibid.
8   Warren J. Blumenfeld and Diane Raymond, *Looking at Gay and Lesbian Life* (Beacon Press, 1989).
9   Elizabeth Moberly, *Homosexuality: A New Christian Ethic* (James Clarke, 1983).
10 D. J. West, *Homosexuality Revisited* (Duckworth, 1977).
11 Blumenfeld and Raymond, *Looking at Gay and Lesbian Life*, op. cit.

12 G. M. Herek in *Encyclopaedia of Psychology* (John Wiley & Sons, 1994).

13 David Engelsma, in the US magazine *The Standard Bearer*, April 1982.

14 E.g. 'The Christian Response to the Gay Agenda', REFORM/Cost of Conscience, 1998.

15 John J. McNeil, 'Homosexuality: Challenging the Church to Grow', *The Christian Century*, March 1987.

16 Letha Dawson Scanzoni, 'Christians and Homosexuality' – a special edition of the US magazine, *The Other Side*, 1994.

17 Adrian Thatcher, *Liberating Sex* (SPCK, 1993).

18 Elizabeth Stuart, *Just Good Friends* (Mowbray, 1995).

19 *Aliens in the Household of God*, ed Paul Germond and Steve de Gruchy, op. cit.

20 Lisa Sowle Cahill in *Homosexuality in the Church*, ed. Jeffrey S. Siker, op. cit.

21 Jones and Workman, op. cit.

22 Jeffrey Satinover, *Homosexuality and the Politics of Truth* (Hamewith Books, 1996).

23 David Greenberg, *The Construction of Homosexuality* (University of Chicago Press, 1988).

24 Rosemary Radford Ruether, quoted in Thatcher, op. cit.

25 Elizabeth Stuart, 'The Development of Queer Theology', *The Way*, October 1999.

26 Vasey, *Strangers and Friends*, op. cit.

Chapter 5: Experience

1 James B. Nelson, *Body Theology*, (Westminster/John Knox Press, 1992).

2 Official Report of the Lambeth Conference (Morehouse Publishing, 1999).

3 'The AIDS Epidemic' in John Stott, *Same Sex Partnerships?* (Marshall Pickering, 1998).

4   John E. Fortunato, *Aids, The Spiritual Dilemma* (Harper & Row, 1987).

5   Kenneth Leech, 'The Carnality of Grace' in *Embracing the Chaos – Theological Responses to AIDS*, ed. James Woodward (SPCK, 1990).

6   A. Nicholas Groth with H. Jean Birnbaum, *Men Who Rape* (New York: Plenum Press, 1976).

7   A. Nicholas Groth, *Sexual Assault of Children and Adolescents* (Lexington Books, 1978).

8   Eric Marcus, *Is it a choice?* (Harper San Francisco, 1993).

9   Alan A. Brash, *Facing our Differences* (World Council of Churches Publications, 1995).

10 James B. Nelson in *Homosexuality in the Church*, ed. Jeffrey S. Siker, op. cit.

11 'Letter to the Bishops of the Catholic Church on the Pastoral Care of Homosexual Persons', Congregation for the Doctrine of the Faith, 1986.

12 Mario Bergner, *Setting Love in Order* (Monarch, 1995).

13 D.C. Haldeman, 'The Practice and Ethics of Sexual Orientation Conversion Therapy', *Journal of Consulting and Clinical Psychology* 62 (1994).

14 John J. McNeil, *The Church and the Homosexual* (Sheed Andrews & McMeel, 1976).

15 Andrew Sullivan, 'Alone Again, Naturally: the Catholic Church and the Homosexual', *The New Republic*, November 1994.

16 *Speaking for Ourselves* (URC Church and Society Department, 1995).

17 *The Other Way?*, Changing Attitudes (1998).

18 Paul Germond in *Aliens in the Household of God*, op. cit.

19 In *Aliens in the Household of God*, op. cit.

20 Vasey, *Strangers and Friends*, op. cit.

21 Private letter, used with permission.

22 Henri J. M. Nouwen, *Sexual Dimensions of the Spiritual Life* (Dublin: Gill & MacMillan, 1979).

23 Michael Ford, *Wounded Prophet: a portrait of Henri J. M. Nouwen* (Darton, Longman & Todd, 1998).

24 Martin L. Smith, SSJE in *Our Selves, Our Souls and Bodies*, ed. Charles Hefling, op. cit.

25 'Letter to the Bishops of the Catholic Church on the Pastoral Care of Homosexual Persons', Congregation for the Doctrine of the Faith, 1986.

26 Two gay priests, in 'The Other Way', Changing Attitudes (1998).

27 John Linscheid, in 'Christians and Homosexuality', a special edition of the US magazine *The Other Side*, 1994.

28 Patrick D. Miller in *Homosexuality and Christian Community*, ed. Choon-Leong Seow, op.cit.

29 Rt Revd Frederick H. Borsch, Bishop of Los Angeles, writing to his diocese on 'Christian Discipleship and Sexuality'.

30 David Scott in *Anglican Theological Review*, 1990.

31 Thatcher, *Liberating Sex*, op. cit.

32 C.S. Lewis, *The Four Loves* (Collins Fontana, 1960).

33 Ian D. Corbett in *Aliens in the Household of God*, op. cit.

34 Dame Julian of Norwich, 'A Revelation of Love', ch. 26: The Twelfth Showing.

35 Marvin M. Ellison in *Sexuality and Gender*, ed. Adrian Thatcher and Elizabeth Stuart (Eerdmans/Gracewing, 1996).

36 Thatcher, *Liberating Sex*, op. cit.

37 Jim Cotter, *Pleasure, Pain and Passion* (Cairns Publications, 1993).

38 Chris Glazer, *Coming Out as Sacrament* (Westminster/John Knox Press, 1998).

39 Rebecca Parker, 'Making Love as a Means of Grace: Women's Reflections' in *Open Hands*, vol. 3, no. 3, Winter 1988.

40 Karen Lebacqz and Ronald G. Barton, *Sex in the Parish* (Westminster/John Knox Press, 1991).

41 'Marriage: a teaching document from the House of Bishops of the Church of England' (1999).

42   'Family Changes: Guide to the Issues' (Family Policy Studies Centre, March 2000).

43   Thatcher, *Liberating Sex*, op. cit.

44   Official Report of the Lambeth Conference 1998 (Morehouse Publishing, 1999).

45   Robert Williams, 'Towards a Theology for Lesbian and Gay Marriage', *Anglican Theological Review*, 1990.

46   Christopher L. Cantlon and Pauline A. Thompson (eds), *'An Honourable Estate': Marriage, Same-Sex Unions, and the Church* (Toronto: Anglican Book Centre, 1997).

47   Andrew Sullivan, *Love Undetectable* (Vintage, 1998).

48   Andrew Sullivan, 'Here comes the Groom', *The New Republic*, August 1989.

49   Charles E. Bennison, Bishop of Pennsylvania, in *Anglican Theological Review*, Fall 1997.

50   Jeffrey John, *'Permanent, Faithful, Stable': Christian Same-sex Partnerships*, (Affirming Catholicism/Darton, Longman & Todd, 1993; new edition 2000).

51   Tony Higton, *Homosexuality and the Church* (ABWON, 1997).

52   Thomas E. Breidenthal, *Christian Households* (Cowley Publications, 1997).

53   Vasey, *Strangers and Friends*, op. cit.

54   2 Samuel 1:26 NRSV.

55   Ruth 1:16f.

56   John 19:26f.

57   Stuart, *Just Good Friends*, op. cit.

58   Ibid.

59   Richard Holloway, *Godless Morality* (Canongate, 1999).

60   Wink (ed.), *Homosexuality and Christian Faith*, op. cit.

Chapter 6: Where Now?

1   Romans 12:1.

2   Matthew 25.

3   Acts 15:13–18.

4   Galatians 3:28.

5   Reproduced in *The Way Forward – Christian Voices on Homo-sexuality and the Church*, ed. Timothy Bradshaw (Hodder & Stoughton, 1997).

6   Alasdair MacIntyre, *After Virtue: a study in moral theology* (Notre Dame University Press, 1981).

7   Rowan Williams, 'Knowing myself in Christ', in *The Way Forward?*, op. cit.

8   Stuart, *Just Good Friends*, op. cit.

9   Jennifer M. Philips, *The Journal of the Association of Anglican Musicians*, March 1999.